INSIDE HORSE RACING

INSIDE HORSE RACING

Jay Hovdey

BALLANTINE BOOKS • NEW YORK

Grateful acknowledgment is made to the following to quote from pre-
viously published material

Los Angeles Times excerpt from an article by Jim Murray in the May 1,
1986 issue of the *Los Angeles Times* Copyright © 1986 by the Los
Angeles Times Syndicate Reprinted with permission

The New York Times excerpt from an article by Steve Crist in the October 3, 1985 issue of *The New York Times* Copyright © 1985 by The
New York Times Company Reprinted by permission

San Diego Tribune excerpt from an article by Jerry Froide from the
August 18, 1981 issue of the *San Diego Tribune* Reprinted courtesy of
the *San Diego Tribune*

St Martin's Press, Inc   excerpt from *Confessions of a Race Track
Fiend* by Maurice Zolotow Copyright © 1983 by Maurice Zolotow. Re-
printed by permission of St Martin's Press, Inc and Richard Curtis
Associates, Inc

Library of Congress Catalog Card Number 86-91565

ISBN 9780345336484

Text design by Gene Siegel
Cover design by Andrew Newman
Cover photo by Joseph Diorio/Equine Images, Inc

Manufactured in the United States of America

First Edition May 1987

146604632

To Suzie and Eddie—winners.

The statistical treasure troves of the *Daily Racing Form* were of invaluable assistance in the compilation of *Inside Horse Racing*. Many thanks to the people at the *Daily Racing Form* who work so hard to publish the past performances, the *American Racing Manual*, the Annual Review Editions, and the Microfiche Monthly Chart Service. In addition, the publicity departments of racetracks from coast to coast helped in many areas of research. And to my statistical soldiers: Thank you Bruce Herman for your creative advice, and thank you Ken Davis for helping me battle the numbers in the trenches.

Contents

INSIDE HORSE RACING

Introduction:
What's in a Number?

I can't figure out a tip at a restaurant. I had to tattoo my automatic teller code on the inside of my left ankle. Just when I'd sorted out my driver's license number from my social security number from my nine-digit zip code, along came a computer mail-drop I.D. number for one publication and a super-secret 800 phone number for another.

I hate numbers.

Unless, of course, they come attached to four legs, a tail, and the majestic head of a thoroughbred, that sweating, snorting, 40-mile-per-hour rogue prince of the animal kingdom. Thoroughbreds can make numbers sing.

No sport, with the possible exception of baseball, can be statistically dissected as completely as thoroughbred racing. Fan's betting depends heavily on numbers—as revealed in the sometimes arcane calculations that are part of handicapping. Breeders mate stallions and mares based on the numerically expressed performances of generations of thoroughbreds long dead. Jockeys and trainers are judged by the health of their numbers more often than for their horsemanship.

Toss out a number and there is a magical story close at its heels. 31! (The number of lengths by which Secretariat won the 1973 Belmont.) 19! (Citation's win total at the end of a remarkable 1948 campaign.) 137! (The weight carried by Forego in his unforgettable '76 Marlboro Cup.) 1:32⅕! (Dr. Fager's unbreakable record for the mile.)

Numbers and their organized cousins—statistics—make evaluating racing much more manageable. Racing fans and handicappers have an especially rough time telling "who's who" among thoroughbreds, since there are no leagues, no schedules, and no required common competition among the top players. Racing has no Super Bowl, no World Series, no formal play-off tournament to determine the best and

1

brightest. Although the majority of horses, jockeys, and trainers tend to stick to mini-circuits that give their lives some stability, there is a vast amount of cross-pollination between regions and states, especially at the top of the game. The racing season lasts from January 1 through December 31, with vast amounts of prize money up for grabs literally every day of the year.

Numbers are the vital infrastructure upon which racing analysts ultimately base their conclusions. A person caught popping off about the "best horse" or the "best jockey" can get hung out to dry if the numbers don't back him up. Quite obviously, the most popular numbers in racing are the winning payoff (for the bettor) and the winning purse (for the owner, trainer and jockey). Run a total of those two columns, do a little cross-checking, and one should be able to isolate racing's best performers. Sounds simple, doesn't it?

Too simple, as a matter of fact. The raw numbers of racing are highly deceiving. Grand totals can be tossed around without regard for such critical variables as efficiency and opportunity. As Darrell Huff puts it in his sardonic masterpiece, *How to Lie With Statistics*, "The only thing wrong is that along with the figures and the facts goes a totally wrong conclusion."

Wrong conclusions. Expensive for the handicapper, embarrassing for the serious fan. The best horse by one set of standards may fall far short by another. One fan's best jockey may be another fan's anchor, depending on the criteria used to judge them. There are too many shades to the panorama of the sport—grass and dirt surfaces, sprints and routes, claimers and classics—to count on grandiose totals or sweeping generalizations for legitimate conclusions.

Informed opinions are valuable and, let's face it, far more entertaining than cold numbers. But to avoid the wrong conclusions, emotional considerations must be eliminated whenever possible. There's nothing wrong with having a favorite horse, trainer, or jockey based upon some very personal standards. But don't mistake them for the "best" until they have passed the test of cold, statistical scrutiny.

Much of the statistical data used in this book comes from the 1985 thoroughbred racing year, the most fully audited and digested season available at the time of this writing. Thoroughbred racing, though geographically widespread and economically diverse, has a useful symmetry when it comes to statistical analysis. In general, everyone accepts the same raw numbers and tabular arrangements. The trick is interpreting those numbers and rearranging those tables to draw the proper conclusions about the who, what, when, and where of being the best.

I could have used any season, really, to illustrate the ways in which excellence is measured in the sport. However, 1985 was a watershed year in many ways. Among the horses, John Henry's career was finally over and Slew O'Gold had been retired, leaving a tremendous void at the top of the sport. In their absence, Spend A Buck proved you could be considered the best without going through the traditional steps. Among the jockeys, the top ranks began to shuffle. The supremacy of Angel Cordero, Laffit Pincay, and Jorge Velasquez was being threatened by a younger generation, led by Jose Santos, Gary Stevens, and Pat Day. And among trainers, the game was permanently altered by the "national" stable of D. Wayne Lukas, who broke nearly every record when it came to winning big money with top horses.

If, through the use of statistics, you can uncover definite tendencies in the records of horses, trainers, jockeys, or even public handicappers, you will improve your chances of making intelligent choices and become a better student of the sport. That is my hope for this book; that is my wish for the reader—because there is no game like thoroughbred racing when it comes to satisfying so many sides of the sporting ego, whether it be the intellect, the heart, or the pocketbook.

So here I stand, equipped with an armful of measuring sticks, ready to tackle racing by the numbers. I hope the serious handicapper will be enlightened by new ways to evaluate horses and people; the casual fan will discover how the stars of racing are born; and those who breed, own, train, and ride thoroughbred horses will consider this a tribute to their sport.

Thinning the Herd: The Horses

1

Any tale of thoroughbred racing, whether it is statistical or only whimsical, must begin with the horse. Trainers and jockeys can only tinker with the raw materials they're given. The horse enters this world with his destiny bound by physical conformation and coordination. A hoof could be turned in or out by only centimeters, or a joint could be set one or two degrees off the ideal angle. These tiny deviations will determine how fast and how far he can run—and how long he will last.

Once the thoroughbred arrives at the racetrack, however, he becomes a puzzle of a different sort. By then he has grown accustomed to his own limitations—what you see is what you get. The horse is no longer rated against an ideal model; he is rated against his peers, based on his record. It is now up to handicappers, racing fans, owners, trainers, and jockeys to interpret the past and invest in the future.

Essentially, followers of the racing game are interested in two different kinds of ratings: First, handicappers earn their daily bread by rating horses race by race, searching for golden opportunities. Owners, breeders, trainers, and journalists, on the other hand, need to rate horses over a longer haul—for history, for the gene pool, and for the survival of personal careers.

Obviously, then, there is plenty of interest in reliable methods of quantifying the quality of a thoroughbred. This chapter will analyze, from several different angles, how horses can be judged. Taking a close look at the various ways racehorses are compared to or rated against each other will help us with our own mundane concerns. After all, there's no better day at the races than a winning day at the races.

The Big Picture

More than 80,000 thoroughbreds will compete in a given year. In 1985 the figure was 82,471. Of those, the general sporting public will

4

pay attention to only one, the Kentucky Derby winner, even though chances are that the Derby winner is not the best of the bunch.

Handicappers and serious racing fans need to do better than that. Fortunately, it's not hard to do.

Certain categories of achievement are widely accepted as natural measuring sticks. All the names and numbers—the records of thoroughbred performance—are right there for everyone to see.

In the best possible world, we should be able to quantify those categories and interpret the results to reveal the name of the best horse in a given situation. It shouldn't matter if we're trying to identify the winner of the fourth race on a Thursday afternoon at Oaklawn Park or the Horse of the Year.

The main factors to consider when rating thoroughbreds are money, speed, consistency, timing, pedigree, and company. Let's take a closer look at them.

Money. Slightly more than 2 percent of all horses will win top-class races, called "sweepstakes" or "stakes" for short. Most of them will be forgotten the moment they cross the finish line. But by winning stakes, those horses at least have added to the amount they end up earning on the racetrack.

And every little bit helps. Racing is either a very expensive hobby or a very serious business. The average cost of training a thoroughbred at a major-league racetrack for a year is over $20,000, which includes daily stall fees, veterinary bills, horseshoeing, insurance, and transportation. Of the 82,471 horses that competed in 1985, only 5 percent earned over $30,000, or enough to cover their costs and provide a small return on the investment.

No one ever said horse racing was an equal-opportunity game. The top 30 money-winning horses of 1985 (making up .03 percent of the racing population), with earnings ranging from Spend A Buck's $3,552,704 to Estrapade's $601,800, banked a cool $29,115,679. That figure represented 4.4 percent of the total prize money offered during the season. In other words, more than 99.9 percent of the horse population had to settle for the "95-cent dollars" left over.

Determining the quality of a racehorse by its bankroll is a widely accepted standard of measurement. It is certainly the American way— the one with the most goodies at the end of the game wins. All nine Eclipse Award winners from 1985 also appeared among the top 25 money-winners. The first thing mentioned about John Henry is that he earned an all-time record $6.5 million, not the fact that he was the only horse in history to win the Santa Anita Handicap twice, a remarkable accomplishment, but far too esoteric for general consumption.

Handicappers should beware of taking earnings too literally, however. Many horses will slip through the cracks of an earnings criterion. Sprinters, for example, will be significantly undervalued. You can count North America's top sprint races without taking off your shoes, and the purses rank well below those offered the long-distance runners. Sometimes a good horse is injured and misses most of a season. His earnings will not necessarily reflect his ability. And then there are the foreign loopholes—watch out for big bucks won in off-brand racing countries, where the competition is often inferior to the North American sport. The best recent example was the Venezuelan mare Trinycarol, who came to the U.S. in 1984 boasting a bankroll of $2.6 million won in puffed-up, sponsored races in Caracas. Trinycarol proceeded to finish last in three American starts before being mercifully retired.

Speed. This is the essence of the sport, and because of that, the most popular handicapping tool. The majority of serious handicappers base their wagers, at least in part, upon a speed rating. A horse's recent record will be boiled down to a number that takes into account final times, track conditions, maintenance of the track, pace of the race, and even such esoteric imponderables as wind, altitude, fog, and time of day. For the casual or beginning handicapper, veterans of the sport offer two warnings: (1) Never overestimate the importance of fast times. (2) A horse isn't necessarily great because he's fast, but a horse has to be fast to be great. (During his three Horse of the Year campaigns, 1974–1976, the great Forego set exactly *one* track record. He did, however, come close to records on several other occasions.)

Consistency. Handicappers (and historians) hate surprises. Aberrations in form must be explained or doubts will linger about a horse forever. Almost as much has been written about Secretariat's three losses in 1973 as his glorious Triple Crown victories.

There are many consolation prizes in racing. In most cases, if a horse loses a race he at least will not have to face the winner in his next start. In major stakes races (the top echelon of events), considerable credit is given for finishing second or third, or even fourth, when a horse is retired to the breeding portion of its career.

Still, for the gambling fan, the most important aspect of consistency is winning. The handicapper must have a certain amount of confidence in how reliably a horse can reproduce his best effort. Part of the art of rating horses is justifying failure. Low points in a horse's record need logical explanations. Sometimes, the handicapper who can accurately dispense with those nagging low points will reap the benefits of higher odds.

Timing. Some horses take Andy Warhol's prediction literally and settle for 15 minutes of fame. Stallions have been syndicated for millions on the strength of one afternoon's work. If the race was the Kentucky Derby, the Belmont Stakes, or the Breeders' Cup Classic, they picked the right afternoon.

Journalists and historians have learned to "throw out" certain races when rating horses. Handicappers should do likewise. In August of 1986, the remarkable little mare Estrapade made two appearances. First, she finished sixth when heavily favored in the $98,300 Palomar Handicap at Del Mar. Three weeks later she won the Budweiser-Arlington Million in Chicago and earned $600,000. The Palomar had been widely advertised as Estrapade's "prep" for the Million, and the public was forewarned in articles leading up to the Del Mar race. The fans chose to bet on the strength of Estrapade's past record—which was outstanding—rather than take into consideration the timing of the race in relation to a far more lucrative future. They paid the price.

Pedigree. Bigotry is alive and well in thoroughbred racing. If a homegrown horse raised in a corner of Arizona fails at the races, all is forgiven. He never really had a chance, did he? But if some brushed and polished baby from a high-rolling Kentucky cradle is a bust, you can hear the bubble pop all around the racing world.

Snow Chief was born in the high desert of California, the son of an old, forgotten stallion and a bargain-basement mare. No one expected great things from him. If he earned his keep, he would have been considered a success. So when he shocked the racing world by leveling all competition early in 1985 and eventually winning the Preakness, he was instantly labeled a genetic freak. The word *fluke* followed Snow Chief wherever he went.

Canadian Bound, on the other hand, was a son of the great Secretariat and the brother of a champion mare named Dahlia. He was bought by a syndicate for $1.5 million (a record at the time) and sent to Europe with highest expectations. He was trained in France by one of the best, Maurice Zilber, and then later shipped to California, where Charlie Whittingham gave it a try. The result? After three years of training and little racing, Canadian Bound had earned $1,050. The syndicate finally decided to cut its considerable losses and retired him to stud in a quiet corner of Kentucky, where he has managed to sire a few horses better than himself . . . which ain't saying much.

Snow Chief, with his pedigree, had everything to gain and nothing to lose, since expectations were accordingly low. Canadian Bound, with his blue blood and high price tag, had everything to lose, and did.

Misleading as it can be, pedigree can be valuable if it is added to the overall mix of the handicapping equation. There are pedigrees—reinforced down through the years and the generations—that lend themselves to sprinting, routing, mud racing, or grass racing. Furthermore, there is a direct correlation between the success of a sire or dam on the racetrack and the tendency to pass on that ability to their offspring.

Some tracks today offer a pedigree analysis in the daily program to help handicappers analyze certain races (primarily maiden races). The service was developed by Jay Woodward, the highly regarded former chartmaker for the *Daily Racing Form*. The brief analysis includes the fee paid for the sire of the horse in question, as well as abbreviated comments on the quality of the dam, and her record as a racehorse and as a producer of racehorses. Believers in such analysis will go so far as to choose a horse fathered by a $40,000 stud over one sired by a $30,000 stud. *Brave New World* meets *My Friend Flicka*.

Company. Going 1 for 4 off Dwight Gooden or forcing the Celtics to six games in a losing cause is a job well done. The only losers in horse racing who get a round of applause are those who have taken on the toughest challenges. In 1979 a giant of a mare named Trillion came over from France and finished second in four straight races. They just happened to be the four toughest turf races on the continent that year. Trillion, without a single North American victory, was named champion of her division. Alydar will always be remembered in the same breath as 1978 Triple Crown winner Affirmed, even though his accomplishments do not compare. Why? Because everytime Affirmed looked over his shoulder, Alydar was breathing down his neck. Everybody loves an underdog, so Alydar became the most popular loser in modern racing history. Without Affirmed, Alydar would have been just another run-of-the-mill Triple Crown champion and Horse of the Year.

Horses carry their past associations with them wherever they go and are judged in terms of the company they keep (or keep up with). The cheap horse on a roll is an especially dangerous creature, as many professionals will attest. He will face tougher and tougher competition until he validates his own version of the Peter Principle, eventually rising to a level at which he proves incompetent. The only problem is, there are folks out there who stand to make or lose money on just when that level of incompetence is reached. The handicapper must be able to place a horse in its proper context to recognize the level at which it can compete. The other factors—money, speed, consistency, timing, and pedigree—tend to follow.

Dancing in the Dark

Why rate horses at all? Why not just sit back and enjoy their grace and style, betting occasionally on the gray one, the black one, or the one whose jockey is wearing red? Pragmatically, handicappers have to be able to assume that the way horses "behave" in a race is not completely random (otherwise, we'd all be better off playing Lotto), that there is some discernible rhyme or reason to the way they ran in the past and will run in the future. And, in another sense, horses must be held accountable for their performances in order to be placed in the panorama of sports history. Picking the champions may not pay off at the betting window, but it is good exercise for the agile sports mind.

The best horses of a season are singled out in a variety of ways. The cream of the crop is honored with Eclipse Awards, which single out nine divisional champions and one supreme champion, the Horse of the Year. The Eclipse Awards have been called the Academy Awards of racing, but that is a misleading comparison. Oscars are handed out by the people who make the movies; Eclipse Awards are determined by the critics.

Selecting Eclipse Award winners is (or should be) a serious responsibility. The ramifications are great. A champion (or even near-champion) will be assessed more weight in subsequent handicap races, which in turn will affect his performance. A champion will draw a disproportionate amount of emotional wagering, the "everybody loves a winner" syndrome. At the same time, a champion will be targeted by rival jockeys and trainers because as much as everybody loves a winner, everybody also wants to knock off No. 1. And, finally, a champion will be valued at a greater rate when sold or syndicated, whether or not his performances truly merit the price tag.

Steve Crist, the respected racing writer for *The New York Times*, worried loudly and in public about the way North America selects its champions. In his *Times* column in the fall of 1985 he observed:

"Just as imperfect [as the criteria for the Horse of the Year honors] are the three voting blocks which have equal say in the title: the National Turf Writers' Association, a group of sportswriters whose membership rolls are filled with retirees and baseball writers whose annual racegoing consists of the Kentucky Derby; selected employees of the *Daily Racing Form*, including chart-callers at obscure tracks in the hinterlands; and racing secretaries at each of the nation's tracks.

"Some of these secretaries are out of touch with racing beyond their local perimeters; others operate from self-interest, hoping to see titles awarded to horses who raced at their tracks, since this might attract better stock in the future."

There has to be a better way.

Performance Rates

There is a numerical beast known as a "Performance Rate" that tries to show which horses rank ahead or behind other horses, based upon demonstrated racetrack ability. It is intended to be a clean, stripped-down method of rating that completely eliminates such subjective variables as speed factors and purse earnings. Hypothetically, these ratings would not only be more scientific than the Eclipse Awards process, but would also provide a valuable aid for the serious handicapper. After all, if there is a magic number that can describe how a horse performs against all competition, in every situation, I'd want to know that number.

Dr. Robert A. Porter of the Spindletop Research Center in Lexington, Kentucky, gets the credit for refining and calculating the Performance Rates. In *The Thoroughbred Record*, an industry publication, Dr. Porter endeavored to explain the mathematics behind the rates. Remember now, this guy's a computer wiz, so don't let him get too far afield. But he's also a lover of thoroughbreds who knows which end of the horse hits the finish line first.

"The basic input to obtaining the measure of 'goodness' of a horse is who he beat—or who beat him—and by how much," Dr. Porter wrote.

"Any race in which the horse has run produces several—and almost certainly conflicting—indications of how good the horse is, one from each of the other horses against which he ran. For example, if he finished several lengths ahead of a good horse, or a few lengths behind a very good horse, he looks good. On the other hand, if a poor horse beat him by several lengths, or if he finished only a few lengths ahead of a very poor horse, he looks bad. The resolution of this conflict, of course, is to take the average of these different estimates of ability, one from each other horse in the race, and to call this average his "performance" in the race.

"In turn, if the horse has run in several races, each race produces a performance, and, horse racing being what it is, these performances will not be the same. Again, the solution is to take the average of his several performances, one from each race in which he has run.

"Why is this a good, or even a sensible criterion for selection? Let us consider why it is that, in a race, it usually happens that one horse wins and a lot of horses lose. One reason obviously is that the racing ability of some horses is better than the racing ability of some other horses. There are lots of other reasons, such as variations in training, like or dislike of the track, jockey's judgment or lack of it, racing luck, hanky-panky, or whatever.

"The objective of the ratings is to measure the horses' racing ability, untempered as much as possible by these other, random (one hopes) influences. Basic reading ability should carry over from race to race. Consequently, it seems logical that the best measure of it is the one that best carries over from race to race."

Dr. Porter also provided a simplified example of the first step in the calculation of Performance Rates.

"First, assume that there are only five horses and one race and that those five horses all finished one length apart. They could then be rated as follows:

Horse #1 +2 lengths
Horse #2 +1 length
Horse #3   0 lengths
Horse #4 −1 length
Horse #5 −2 lengths

"Now assume a second race in which Horse #2 plus four others run, and that they, too, (for simplicity) all finish one length apart. Again, rating the horses in this race as if there were no other horses or races:

Horse #6 +2 lengths
Horse #7 +1 length
Horse #8   0 lengths

Horse #2 −1 length
Horse #9 −2 lengths

"Through Horse #2, which ran in both races, there is now a basis for comparing the two races and developing a common rating for all of the horses.

"Horse #2, the link between the races, was two lengths worse in race number two than in race number one. *Therefore, all of the ratings for race number two, if increased by two lengths, would be on the same scale as the ratings for race number one* [my italics]. The first recalculation of the ratings of the horses in race number two would be:

Horse #6 +4 lengths
Horse #7 +3 lengths
Horse #8 +2 lengths
Horse #2 +1 length
Horse #9   0 lengths

"Because all are now on a common scale [based on Horse #2], the ratings of all the horses, from best to worst, are:

Horse #6 +4 lengths
Horse #7 +3 lengths
Horse #8 +2 lengths
Horse #1 +2 lengths
Horse #2 +1 length
Horse #9   0 lengths
Horse #3   0 lengths
Horse #4 −1 length
Horse #5 −2 lengths"

Each year *The Thoroughbred Record* publishes Performance Rates for the top horses that raced in the previous year, and each year the results create a predictable stir. A few surprises always creep into the six divisional categories—horses which have been overlooked by such traditional measures as the Eclipse Awards, *Daily Racing Form* Free Handicap, Jockey Club Experimental Handicap, and *The Blood-Horse* Free Handicap, which is sponsored by *The Record*'s chief magazine rival.

Timothy Capps, editor of *The Record*, offered a kind of "product warning" when the 1985 Performance Rates were published in April of 1986.

"Performance Rates are not represented as being the ultimate answer to the riddle of whose horse is the best horse," he wrote. "They are, however, a wonderful device for measuring performance without regard to earnings or the many subjective variables that enter into an individual race. . . . Draw your own conclusions and argue about them at will. Remember one thing about Performance Rates or any other rating system: they are purely a function of past performances and may or may not have great value in forecasting future events. That uncertainty is why we keep racing horses."

So here are the top 10 horses in each Performance Rate category of 1985, based on sex and age. Turf, dirt, or sprint specialists were not differentiated. Older horses and 3-year-olds with fewer than three starts (in this country) were not rated, which eliminated such accomplished European performers as Pebbles, Rousillon, Shadeed, and Teleprompter. For a 2-year-old to be rated, it must have started at least four times. Therefore, Ogygian, Meadowlake, and Swear (undefeated 2-year-olds who, because of injury or death were out of the picture early) were not included.

2-Year-Old Males	PR	2-Year-Old Females	PR
Admiral's Image	24.9	Twilight Ridge	24.9
Mogambo	24.1	I'm Sweets	24.2
Pillaster	23.9	*Family Style	24.1
Storm Cat	23.9	Guadery	23.7
Hilco Scamper	23.1	I'm Splendid	22.7
Ketoh	22.8	Nervous Baba	22.3
*Tasso	22.7	Steal a Kiss	22.1
Roy	21.9	Musical Lark	22.0
Papal Power	21.6	Toes Knows	21.2
Snow Chief	21.2	Funistrada	20.8

3-Year-Old Males	PR	3-Year-Old Females	PR
*Spend A Buck	29.2	*Mom's Command	28.9
Chief's Crown	27.2	Kamikaze Rick	25.8
Proud Truth	26.7	Majestic Folly	24.0
Rhoman Rule	26.4	Shocker T.	22.8
Stephan's Odyssey	25.8	Jolly Saint	22.7
Another Reef	25.2	Lady's Secret	22.4
Smile	24.2	Fran's Valentine	22.1
Phone Trick	23.9	Favorable Review	21.7
Tank's Prospect	23.8	Self Image	21.6
Creme Fraiche	23.7	Duty Dance	21.5

Older Males	PR	Older Females	PR
*Vanlandingham	26.8	Heatherten	25.3
Gate Dancer	25.3	Percipient	23.6
**Precisionist	24.8	*Life's Magic	23.3
Greinton	24.7	Key Dancer	22.9
Carr de Naskra	24.6	Mitterand	22.7
Strawberry Road	24.6	Possible Mate	21.5
Track Barron	24.3	Sefa's Beauty	21.0
Garthorn	23.8	Isayso	20.5
Stay the Course	23.8	Dowery	20.3
Bob Back	23.2	Dontstop Themusic	20.0

* Division champion
** Sprint division champion

Meanwhile, here I sit in my glass house, just itching to get at a pile of stones. How can a system that rates Percipient over Mitterand be taken seriously? Percipient finished second in each of her three 1985 races, all of them won by Mitterand. Gate Dancer won exactly one race—in Nebraska!—and we are asked to believe he was a better performer than either Greinton (who beat him three times) or Precisionist (who beat him twice). Shocker T. was the queen of Calder, but that's a far cry from New York, where Lady's Secret became the first filly in history to sweep the prestigious Maskett, Ruffian, and Beldame. And thank God for Admiral's Image. Even though he was never mentioned in the same breath as Tasso, Ogygian, or Snow Chief (the first three in Eclipse balloting), he saved the magazine from the nasty coincidence of Mogambo and Pillaster leading the list of 2-year-old colts. Both of them raced for Peter M. Brant, who later bought a controlling interest in *The Thoroughbred Record*.

Performance Rates have a tendency to reward big fish in small ponds (e.g., Admiral's Image, Shocker T.). If a mediocre animal consistently de-feats other mediocre animals, who in turn beat up on another batch of non-entities, then the horse at the top of the pile gets a Performance Rate that does not reflect his overall quality.

In its weakness lies its strength, however. In many cases, horses perceived to be close in quality are parallel lines that never intersect. The 2-year-old fillies I'm Sweets and I'm Splendid offer a perfect illustration of how Performance Rates can cut through disproportionate purses and juggle similar records into a final, fair appraisal.

I'm Sweets had a record of seven starts, three wins, two seconds, and one third and earnings of $312,518. I'm Splendid had a similar mark of 7—4—1—0—and earnings of $560,857 ($344,217 of it won in a single race, the Hollywood Starlet). Both fillies were Grade I (the best) race winners, and they had many of the best in their division as common foes, including Twilight Ridge, Family Style, Musical Lark, and Steal a Kiss. Only thing was, they never faced each other.

On closer inspection, the Performance Rate calculations discovered that I'm Sweets raced well against slightly tougher company on a regular basis. A look at the charts from each of the 14 races bears out the findings. I'm Splendid's seven races were populated by 14 fillies that either won a graded stakes or placed in a Grade I stakes during the year. The number for I'm Sweets was 19. Score one for the Performance Rates.

Painting by the Numbers

Pro football had a good idea. (No, not the Cowboy cheerleaders.) The "Passer Rating System," published weekly throughout the season, endeavors to present a complete picture of each quarterback and then grade them according to all-around excellence in numbers that stand up to historical comparison. If a quarterback threw an inordinate amount of interceptions, he was not necessarily doomed to the bottom of the standings. He could salvage those bad numbers with a high score in another category. The four measures used to come up with the ratings are percentage of completions, percentage of touchdown passes, percentage of interceptions, and average yards gained per pass attempt.

A National Football League committee spent three years devising this formula. They came up with a system that boasts numbers for the ages. The Dan Marino of 1986 can be compared with the Fran Tarkenton of 1975 with absolute confidence. Of more interest is the weekly update published in sports pages across the nation which either damns or praises the hometown quarterback.

For instance, a few weeks into the 1985 NFL season, the passing leaders looked like this:

	PA	PC	Pct.	Yds.	Avg.	TD	Int.	Rating
McMahon	123	79	64.2	1,194	9.71	10	5	106.2
Fouts	123	75	61.0	1,084	8.81	10	4	103.2
Bartkowski	111	89	62.2	738	6.65	5	1	92.8
Montana	172	106	61.6	1,273	7.40	10	5	91.5
Esiason	109	64	58.7	762	6.99	7	3	90.1

Six weeks later the top five had a much different profile:

	PA	PC	Pct.	Yds.	Avg.	TD	Int.	Rating
O'Brien	320	196	61.3	2,553	7.98	18	6	97.3
Montana	331	200	60.4	2,293	6.93	16	6	89.9
McMahon	231	136	58.9	1,796	7.77	13	7	89.7
Esiason	299	175	58.5	2,201	7.36	17	8	89.3
Fouts	303	177	58.4	2,446	8.07	19	12	88.8

Racehorses can be rated in much the same way. First, performance categories must be established. Then those categories must be weighted in terms of their degree of impact upon overall performance. Finally, a formula must be devised that assigns each horse a rating number. Ideally, such a rating system could be used any time to sort out the best and worst in a group of horses.

Our rating system uses five categories of racing excellence. They are:

1. *Class.* The quality of each race must be defined by the number of quality horses running. Such a "class pool" of horses can vary in composition, depending on the types of horses being rated. It is unreasonable to expect allowance horses to be competing against Grade I stakes winners, or claimers to mix it up with allowance and stakes horses. This *class* figures will represent the average number of quality individuals (including the horse in question, if he qualifies) that have run in each race on the horse's record. For example, 27 quality individuals present in the fields of a 10-race campaign reflect a class figure of 2.70.

2. *Cream.* A horse should not be blamed if other good horses fail to show up for a big race. The cream component of the class figure gives a horse credit for winning graded races and, to a lesser extent, competing in them at all. (Filly A runs in five graded races and wins two. She gets .400 for her win percentage in those races, plus .100 for each of the five graded races on her record. Her cream figure is .400 + .500, or .900.)

3. *1–2–3.* Wins of any kind are worth .6 of a point, seconds are worth .3, and thirds are worth .1. Anything worse than third is of little use to the public, although, as incentive, owners are paid for lower placings. A perfect score in this category is .600.

4. *$$$$$.* Money matters, no manner where or how it is earned, and the richest races usually attract the best horses. An earnings-per-start figure should be expressed in numbers as close to 1.000 as possible

to keep it in line with the other categories. (Average earnings of $89,065 translates into a $$$$$ figure of .891.)

5. *Load*. Weight is of debatable influence, but its measurement is exact. To reward heavy weight carriers, especially in the handicap divisions, the load factor cannot be ruled out. To keep its marginal impact in proportion to other more important figures, the average weight a horse carries over the course of a season is expressed in thousandths. (Horse B packs 120, 125, 122, 126, and 128 in his five races for a load figure of .124.)

It would be inaccurate to give each of the five categories equal leverage in the final ratings. So, with the input of handicappers and racing statisticians, the calculations were customized to properly reflect the realities of racing, as follows:

Step 1. Cream is a component of the class figure. Add Nos. 1 and 2.

Step 2. 1–2–3 performance must be considered in terms of class and cream. Multiply No. 3 by the sum of 1 and 2.

Step 3. The accumulation of $$$$$ stands alone, as does the load a horse carries. Add Nos. 4 and 5 to the figure from Step 2. That is the final rating.

Here are sample calculations of the final ratings for a pair of 3-year-olds: Creme Fraiche, winner of the Belmont Stakes, and Banner Bob, winner of the Jim Beam Stakes. They each started 15 times during the season but met only twice, and Banner Bob won both decisions. Did that make Banner Bob the better horse in 1985? First, the calculations, then the verdict.

BANNER BOB

Class: 36 top company or "class pool" horses in 15 races.

$$36/15 = 2.40$$

Cream: 11 graded race starts and 4 graded race wins.

$$(4/11) + (11 \times .1) = 1.464$$

1–2–3: 15 starts, 6 wins, 4 seconds, 2 thirds.

$$(6 \times .6) + (4 \times .3) + (2 \times .1) = .333$$

$$$$: Earned $551,578 in 15 starts.

$$551,578/15 = 36,772 \text{ (.368 for formula)}$$

Load: Carried weights of 123, 121, 118, 120, 117, 122, 122, 123, 124, 126, 121, 121, 122, 114, and 121.

$$1,815 \text{ lbs./15} = 121 \text{ (.121 for formula)}$$

Final Rating:
$$(2.40 + 1.46) \times .333 + (.368 + .121) = 1.77$$

CREME FRAICHE

Class: 60 top company horses in 15 races.

$$60/15 = 4.00$$

Cream: 13 graded race starts and 5 graded race wins.

$$(5/13) + (13 \times .1) = 1.685$$

1–2–3: 15 starts, 5 wins, 5 seconds, 3 thirds.

$$(5 \times .6) + (5 \times .3) + (3 \times .1) = .320$$

$$$$: Earned $1,291,397 in 15 starts.

$$1,291,397/15 = 86,093 \text{ (.861 for formula)}$$

Load: Carried weights of 122, 126, 121, 126, 124, 126, 123, 126, 126, 119, 120, 117, 117, 114, and 121.

$$1,828 \text{ lbs./15} = 121.8 \text{ (.122 for formula)}$$

Final Rating:

$$(4.00 + 1.69) \times .320 + (.861 + .122) = 2.80$$

Even though Banner Bob defeated Creme Fraiche in their only two encounters of 1985, the ratings still declare Creme Fraiche the better horse based on the level of his overall competition, the quality of races in which he ran, and the money he won.

The Great Unequalizer

Time! My God, he's left out time! While Americans are obsessed with the passage of time, Europeans are not. That is why speed ratings and track variants do not appear in foreign past-performance lines. And until North American racehorses run over universal surfaces with identical maintenance in uniform weather conditions, final time should not be a factor in determining which horse is the best horse at a given point in history. Always remember Pleasure Shack.

Once he had a touch of class, old Pleasure Shack. But injuries caught up with him and by the age of 8 he ended up in claiming races. One rainy February 8 at Santa Anita in 1981, Pleasure Shack was running in the first race, a 6-furlong event for $25,000 claimers. The track had been rolled hard to keep the water out and the times fast, which is the standard policy of all West Coast tracks.

The fastest 6 furlongs Pleasure Shack had ever run was a 1:09 at the age of 3. Well, a few steps out of the gate that day and he felt like a kid again. With Sandy Hawley just holding on, Pleasure Shack splashed through the first quarter mile in :21⅕, and the half-mile in :43⅖. At that point Santa Anita executives turned white and braced for public embarrassment. As Pleasure Shack bounded down the stretch, on his way to a Santa Anita record 1:07⅗, the track superintendent was getting his ears burned. "Dig up the track!" they screamed. "We don't want a record in every claiming race!" Not even the most sophisticated track variant could have brought Pleasure Shack's clocking in line with reality that day. And he never came close to running even a 1:08 again, let alone a 1:07⅗.

For nearly two years, Pleasure Shack's singular accomplishment appeared at the top of each 6-furlong race on the Santa Anita program. Then, on December 26, 1982, a world-class speedball named Chinook Pass came along and took Santa Anita off the hook by winning the Palos Verdes Handicap in 1:07⅗ over a fast but fair surface. Pleasure Shack became an unperson overnight. His name disappeared from the list of track record-holders. Santa Anita officials redefined his clocking as "not legitimate." The Santa Anita official media guide lists two or more horses holding track records at 4, 5, and 6½ furlongs, a mile and one-sixteenth, and two miles. But there is only one name beside the 6-furlong record: Chinook Pass.

To its credit, the *Daily Racing Form* did not go along with the warped version of history. Its custom is to call the first horse the record-setter, no matter what the circumstances, and list only his name in the track record box. All others are "record-equalers." Pleasure Shack has the last word, at least until a horse comes along with a 1:07⅖.

Pleasure Shack is not an isolated instance. Though a valuable tool, final times have proven a misleading measurement. We have been asked to believe that certain horses are superior because they are running especially fast times. Never mind that they are allowed to run freely on their own, without early challenge to their competitive spirit. And never mind that their opposition may be suspiciously lacking in credentials.

A colt named Groovy was considered the fastest thing under a saddle in the autumn of 1986. He was famous on both coasts for sprinting to the front and never looking back. His clockings were universally fast, by any measurement. Hence, it was no surprise that Groovy was the lowest-priced favorite of the day on the Breeders' Cup program at Santa Anita Park.

So what happened? Groovy was taken by the throat right from the start of his race, and for the first time in his life he failed to make the lead at any point in a race. Groovy, it turned out, had very little stomach for adversity. Groovy was spectacular when running against the clock. But on the day he didn't get things his own way he ran the worst sprint race of his life. The study of time could never account for such a strange twist.

The arguments between proponents of time handicapping and class handicapping have been going on for years. Our ratings system, obviously, favors the class side of the coin to the exclusion of speed influences. "Class" is the map of the thoroughbred world and, rightfully, the clock can be considered a faithful compass. But even before there were compasses, we were able to follow the sun and the stars to find our way home.

Sorting It Out

Remember, any group of horses can be rated or compared, as long as the criteria used by a handicapper or historian are consistent. Let's test our ratings system, focusing upon the best horses to run in North America in 1985. But which ones were the best? Since I've got the word processor, I get to draw the line. Our "best" of 1985 will be culled from the three following groups. To survive the final cut, a horse must make two of the three lists:

Graded stakes winners. Graded, as in report card, *not* mountain roads. In 1986 these represented approximately .5 percent of all races run in North America. A blue-ribbon committee decides which of the more than 1,000 stakes races run each year should be blessed with "graded" status (either I, II, or III).

Grade I–placed horses. Of the 401 graded races run in North America in 1986, 116 were designated "Grade I." As the title suggests, these are the most famous events and, supposedly, the toughest to win. They include the Triple Crown, the Breeders' Cup Series, the Budweiser Million, the Jockey Club Gold Cup, and such regional treasures as the Santa Anita Handicap in California, the Arkansas Derby, the Blue Grass Stakes in Kentucky, the Widener Handicap in Florida, and the United Nations Handicap at Atlantic City. Finishing first, second, or third in Grade I races is an achievement in itself.

Year-end "handicaps." Here subjective opinion raises its ugly head; fortunately, the opinions are usually well grounded. Expert panels made up of well-known racing secretaries (the people who create the races) compare long lists of horses from different parts of the country and develop rankings—expresed as hypothetical weights to be carried in an imaginary competition. To be rated within 10 pounds of the top horse in a year-end handicap is worthy of note.

Each of these categories has its weak spots. Some Grade III races are won by woefully undignified horses who promptly disappear from view. Even an occasional Grade I field can come up pitifully light on quality and/or quantity. In 1985, Hawthorne Park near Chicago inherited the Grade I Secretariat Stakes from crosstown neighbor Arlington Park, which had burned to the ground less than a month before. Only one of the 12 Secretariat entrants had ever placed in a Grade I event; and, by the end of the year, only two of them had won a graded race. Yet the 1-2-3 finishers were granted entry into the Grade I club, right alongside the first three horses across the line in the Kentucky Derby.

Graded races are also overloaded to the East. Politics and tradition play a key role in keeping the West far behind. Among the 12-member committee that graded the 1986 stakes, only one person could be considered from the West. Who could be surprised to find that there were 198 races in eastern seaboard states given graded status, while California, Washington, and Arizona received 122.

The handicaps sometimes miss obvious candidates in an effort to include too many horses. A strutting, handsome colt named Shadeed was omitted from the list of 1985's top 3-year-olds because he had the poor taste to finish fourth in his only North American appearance, the Breeders' Cup Mile (Shadeed was actually moved to third after a disqualification). Back home in England, where he was considered the country's finest miler, Shadeed was rated six pounds superior to the next best horse in his division. His troubled performance in the Breeders' Cup Mile (he was beaten 2¼ lengths by subsequent champion Cozzene) did little to tarnish his European reputation, but nothing at all to enhance his American profile.

In the case of a horse like Shadeed, Thomas S. Robbins, the racing secretary of Santa Anita Park and Del Mar, explained that the weighting committee usually prefers to consider individuals with more North American form. There was, however, an omission of considerably greater embarrassment to Robbins, who was a member of the committee that compiled the 1985 Free Handicap for *The Blood-Horse* magazine.

"We left off a 3-year-old named Nostalgia's Star," said Robbins. "Lost him off the bottom of the list when it was copied."

Nostalgia's Star was a useful runner that season, a winner of two small stakes races. Also, he just happened to be owned by Robbins's father and trained by his brother. Whoops!

Hopefully, the design of this ratings system makes it possible to account for such mistakes and makes sure that horses get credit where credit is due. The handicapper must always be on the lookout for inflated reputations, deceptive performances, and misleading numbers— the trick is to eliminate these false indications and to identify reliable, consistent, high-quality picks.

Out of the 80,000 thoroughbreds who raced in 1985, a total of 191 horses qualified for our study group. By the nature of their qualifications, these are the top 191 horses who raced in 1985, with very few exceptions. At the same time, these 191 horses form our "class pool." The more often a horse ran against members of that pool, the higher his class rating will be.

The nine Eclipse Award categories provide a sensible breakdown of the 191 study group horses, so let's dive in, beginning with our final ratings for the 2-year-old males of 1985:

2-YEAR-OLD MALES

Name	Class	Cream	1-2-3	$$$$$	Load	Final
Meadowlake	2.00	1.100	.600	1.468	.122	3.45
*Tasso	2.43	1.300	.486	1.088	.119	3.02
Storm Cat	2.83	.700	.450	.928	.119	2.64
Ogygian	2.33	1.100	.600	.397	.119	2.57
Snow Chief	2.00	.967	.411	1.040	.119	2.38
Electric Blue	2.33	.100	.500	.790	.119	2.12
Hilco Scamper	1.67	.967	.500	.382	.120	1.82
Pillaster	1.00	.700	.525	.621	.117	1.63
Ketoh	3.25	.633	.300	.330	.121	1.62
Papal Power	2.83	.650	.317	.337	.121	1.56
Swear	1.00	1.100	.600	.181	.118	1.56
Scat Dancer	2.17	.100	.333	.621	.118	1.49
Mogambo	3.00	.650	.257	.429	.120	1.49
Groovy	3.80	.400	.240	.272	.119	1.40
Danzig Connection	2.50	.200	.350	.198	.120	1.26
Sovereign Don	2.11	1.129	.278	.220	.120	1.24
Darby Fair	1.75	.633	.300	.243	.119	1.08
Ferdinand	1.80	.100	.220	.357	.118	0.89
Southern Appeal	1.30	1.100	.160	.178	.118	0.68

* Division champion

Immediate chaos! Eclipse Award voters had it wrong. Meadowlake, a Secretariat look-a-like who went 2 for 2 before an injury knocked him out, was narrowly the ratings choice over champion Tasso, winner of the Breeders' Cup Juvenile and two other major stakes. Storm Cat, who comes next, lost only one race all year—to Tasso. Ogygian is in the Meadowlake category, winning all three of his races impressively before hurting himself. Meadowlake, however, had the good sense to run his best race when a first prize of $286,320 was at stake in the Arlington-Washington Futurity.

The ratings for 1985 2-year-old males say a lot about how we define quality in young horses. Meadowlake, Ogygian, and Swear represent those flashfire personalities that light up the stage for a brilliant few minutes. Seattle Slew, a champion at 2 from the impact of only three starts, is the shining example of their kind. Tasso and Snow Chief, the leading money-winner of the division, represent the less glamorous side of the equation. They were not especially exciting at first, but when all the dust cleared they were the only ones standing at the end of the season.

This is a good spot to drop in a wild card. Testing the validity of the study group, we look at Admiral's Image, a 2-year-old gelding who unreeled a perfect 5-for-5 season in Pennsylvania. None of the three stakes he won was graded, and his average earnings figure was a runty .302. The class/cream figure was 1.20, lowest of any on the list. Granted, the ratings formula is stacked against a horse like Admiral's Image. But the question persists: Was he ever really tested?

Admiral's Image, the division leader in Performance Rates, faced 28 different opponents during the season, 17 of which never so much as finished third in the most insignificant stakes event. Of the rest, two won small stakes, six were stakes placed, and three had graded race credentials. Burdened by such meager company, even with his perfect record, Admiral's Image receives a 1.14 rating, well down the list.

Never count out a low-rated 2-year-old, however. Young horses, particularly colts, undergo tremendous changes as they mature into 3-year-olds. Projections of 1986 form were not intended to be a residual benefit of the ratings. Any predictions would have been foolhardy regarding this particular crop. Primarily because of injuries, Meadowlake, Tasso, and Storm Cat could not continue their form into the next campaign. Only one horse in the ratings' top 10, Preakness Stakes winner Snow Chief, finished in the money in a 1986 Triple Crown event. Ferdinand, obviously, was very much a work-in-progress during his juvenile campaign (.89 rating), and blossomed to win the Kentucky Derby the following spring. Danzig Connection, rated at 1.26, triumphed in the 1986 Belmont Stakes.

On to the next division.

2-YEAR-OLD FILLIES

Name	Class	Cream	1-2-3	$$$$$	Load	Final
Twilight Ridge	3.40	.967	.440	1.271	.118	3.31
*Family Style	3.90	1.175	.370	.806	.118	2.80
I'm Splendid	3.00	1.100	.386	.801	.117	2.50
I'm Sweets	3.86	.900	.329	.446	.118	2.13
Arewehavingfunyet	2.44	1.100	.378	.529	.117	1.98
Lazer Show	1.00	1.100	.600	.526	.117	1.90
Musical Lark	4.14	.767	.300	.243	.117	1.83
Guadery	2.80	.700	.380	.236	.117	1.68
Funistrada	4.50	.300	.225	.356	.119	1.55
Silent Account	3.14	.650	.300	.289	.119	1.55

Name	Class	Cream	1-2-3	$$$$$	Load	Final
Trim Colony	2.40	.200	.380	.421	.118	1.53
Steal A Kiss	3.50	.400	.225	.293	.117	1.29
Parquill	1.00	1.100	.433	.259	.117	1.21
Cosmic Tiger	1.38	.700	.463	.193	.117	1.27
Nervous Baba	2.83	.650	.267	.160	.117	1.21
Really Fancy	2.00	.700	.300	.129	.118	1.06
Pamela Key	2.00	.100	.325	.204	.118	1.01
Deep Silver	1.40	.100	.420	.222	.118	0.97
Laz's Joy	1.50	.100	.213	.143	.116	0.52
Cadabra Abra	1.27	.700	.164	.067	.116	0.51

* Division champion

Twilight Ridge's most important victory came in the Breeders' Cup Juvenile Fillies event when she defeated runner-up Family Style by one length. It was the only time they ran against each other all season long, which is no surprise since they both were owned by Eugene V. Klein and trained by D. Wayne Lukas.

Eclipse Award voters, however, chose to honor Family Style for her consistently admirable performances in top company (she did have the highest class/cream figure of the division, a 5.075, compared to 4.367 for Twilight Ridge). Even though Family Style lost 6 of her 10 starts, she was worse than third only once, and three of her victories came in Grade I events. The hard work ethic pays off once again.

Note that the rankings of I'm Splendid and I'm Sweets reverse their Performance Rate evaluations. With superior 1-2-3 and $$$$$ figures, I'm Splendid was able to overcome the better class/cream figure of her close rival. And they seemed fated to duel forever on paper. Halfway through their 3-year-old season of 1986 they had yet to meet in battle.

The ratings for 2-year-old fillies can be mingled with those for 2-year-old males to form a panoramic view of the entire generation. Although the colts and fillies do not have many common opponents, each group had an opportunity to run for approximately the same amount in purses and in the same number of graded races. The only real disparity is in the weight carried, and that was minimal.

Meadowlake rates atop the entire crop of 1983, with the filly Twilight Ridge close behind. She in turn ranks ahead of both Tasso, the male champion, and Family Style, the filly champion. A significant validation of just such an alignment took place on Breeders' Cup day when Twilight Ridge ran faster in her victory—by one-fifth of a second—than did Tasso in his.

3-YEAR-OLD MALES

Name	Class	Cream	1-2-3	$$$$$	Load	Final
*Spend A Buck	4.43	1.100	.486	2.218	.123	5.03
Proud Truth	4.18	1.456	.436	1.752	.121	4.33
Chief's Crown	5.08	1.344	.350	1.059	.123	3.43
Tank's Prospect	4.57	1.100	.350	1.059	.123	3.40
Creme Fraiche	4.00	1.685	.320	.861	.122	2.80
Skywalker	4.80	.650	.300	.582	.121	2.33
Skip Trial	3.07	1.555	.307	.638	.120	2.18
Rhoman Rule	4.75	.633	.325	.301	.120	2.17
Stephan's Odyssey	4.50	1.282	.258	.504	.123	2.12
Smile	2.67	.933	.322	.590	.122	1.87
Imperial Choice	2.25	.633	.425	.483	.122	1.83
Banner Bob	2.40	1.464	.333	.368	.121	1.77
Eternal Prince	3.70	.933	.250	.415	.122	1.70
Turkoman	2.62	.843	.277	.464	.117	1.52
Encolure	2.71	.800	.257	.304	.121	1.33
Fast Account	4.13	.700	.188	.206	.122	1.24
El Basco	3.75	1.191	.150	.312	.121	1.17
Minutes Away	1.09	1.100	.418	.133	.116	1.16
Padua	1.71	.700	.314	.232	.118	1.11
Image of Greatness	2.50	.700	.225	.262	.120	1.10
Important Business	3.45	.925	.145	.264	.118	1.02
Don's Choice	1.58	.650	.325	.128	.115	0.97
Nostalgia's Star	2.69	1.191	.156	.215	.119	0.94
Government Corner	1.54	.650	.300	.132	.118	0.91
Floating Reserve	3.14	1.000	.143	.150	.119	0.86
Irish Sur	2.78	.700	.111	.205	.118	0.71

* Division champion.

Spend A Buck's earnings for 1985 will be eternally recorded as $3,552,704, which is hogwash, because $2,000,000 of that amount came in bonus form after he won the Jersey Derby. That's like counting Reggie Jackson's endorsements when reporting his baseball salary.

So, for rating purposes, the $2,000,000 was subtracted from Spend A Buck's total, bringing his earnings-per-start figure back into the realm of sanity. You can see what a dramatic effect it had upon his final evaluation . . . still No. 1.

Proud Truth's victory in the $3,000,000 Breeders' Cup Classic, the richest race of the year, carried him over Chief's Crown into second spot on the final ratings. This is somewhat deceptive, since Chief's Crown defeated Proud Truth two of the three times they met; but it also points to the peculiar penchant Chief's Crown had for blowing the big ones. He failed as the favorite in the Kentucky Derby (third), Preakness (second), Belmont Stakes (third), and Breeders' Cup Classic (fourth), perhaps the four most important races for a 3-year-old with championship aspirations. If it is any consolation to fans of Chief's Crown, however, he still would have been rated second had the Derby finish been different. A hypothetical Derby victory lifts Chief's Crown to a 4.04, while a Derby second drops Spend A Buck to 4.26. Had Chief's Crown won the Breeders' Cup Classic his final rating would have been 4.74, still not enough to overtake Spend A Buck's 5.03.

The impression persists that Proud Truth, the leggy chestnut owned by John Galbreath, had a one-race season—the Breeders' Cup Classic—and accomplished little else. Wrong. His campaign was highly successful even without the $1,350,000 payday. Had he lost that photo-finish to Gate Dancer in the Classic, Proud Truth would have earned a 3.52 year-end rating, still second best to Spend A Buck and ahead of Chief's Crown, Preakness winner Tank's Prospect, and Belmont Stakes winner Creme Fraiche.

The ideal rating system should also be able to compare horses of different years, just as the NFL quarterback ratings do with players from various eras. (For example, Ken Stabler's 103.7 in 1976 is one of the all-time highest ratings, but still not as good as Bart Starr's 105.1 in 1966.) Bickering can be half the fun, but perhaps a note of logic can be interjected when racing fans rave on and on about who was better: Man o' War or Citation, Swaps or Nashua, Spectacular Bid or Affirmed.

Let us compare, for instance, the 3-year-old champions of the 1980s. Two minor modifications are necessary in the ratings formula. The earnings-per-start figures have been adjusted using the Consumer Price Index (in 1985 it took $131 to buy what $100 bought in 1980). And, since new races are added to the list of graded stakes every year, the 1985 roster of graded races will be applied retroactively to each season to determine class and cream figures. The compilation of year-end handicaps and traditional amounts of weight carried have remained unchanged. Here are the results:

Name (Year)	Class	Cream	1-2-3	$$$$$	Load	Final
Spend A Buck (85)	4.43	1.100	.486	2.218	.123	5.03
Pleasant Colony (81)	7.11	1.344	.344	1.153	.124	4.19
Swale (84)	4.43	1.267	.400	1.616	.124	4.02
Slew O'Gold (83)	4.58	1.400	.358	.794	.122	3.06
Conquistador Cielo (82)	3.11	1.300	.478	.526	.119	2.75
Temperence Hill (80)	3.18	1.617	.341	.868	.121	2.62

Adjusting for inflation, Temperence Hill's earnings for 1980 were $1,475,816, only $76,888 less than Spend A Buck's bankroll in 1985. Temperence Hill, however, needed 17 races to accumulate his fortune, hence his low $$$$$ figure and subsequent low rating compared to the top names. Temperence Hill won the championship for the same reason Chief's Crown lost it—performance in the most prestigious events with the most exposure. While he failed in such lesser-known races as the Dwyer, Saranac, and Jim Dandy, Temperence Hill won the Belmont Stakes, Travers Stakes, and Jockey Club Gold Cup, all nationally televised.

Though he was not the same kind of money-making machine as was Spend A Buck, 1981 Derby and Preakness winner Pleasant Colony faced substantially tougher fields, as noted by his class figure of 7.11. A higher $$$$$ figure would have put him right beside Spend A Buck at the top of the list.

Along those lines, a case could be made that Pleasant Colony did not have the opportunity to run in a race like the $1,000,000 Jersey Derby (won by Spend A Buck) and therefore should not be penalized. But personalities must be taken into consideration when playing the "what if" game. Pleasant Colony was owned by Thomas Mellon Evans, a man of the old school who would never pass up a chance to win the Triple Crown. After winning the Kentucky Derby, Pleasant Colony would have run in the Preakness whether or not a Jersey Derby existed, no matter what the size of the purse. Spend A Buck, owned by racing newcomer Dennis Diaz, did just the opposite. To carry the idea one step further, had Spend A Buck run in and won the Preakness instead of the Jersey Derby in 1985, his final rating would have been 4.78, still tops among the decade's 3-year-old champs.

3-YEAR-OLD FILLIES

Name	Class	Cream	1-2-3	$$$$$	Load	Final
*Mom's Command	2.67	1.433	.533	.699	.121	3.01
Fran's Valentine	3.50	1.456	.400	.657	.120	2.76
Lady's Secret	2.53	1.500	.441	.585	.119	2.41
Kamikaze Rick	2.50	.967	.517	.363	.116	2.27
Savannah Slew	2.25	.700	.413	.251	.117	1.59
Koluctoo's Jill	2.92	1.175	.262	.268	.119	1.46
Marshua's Echelon	1.67	.700	.400	.290	.119	1.36
Bessarabian	2.00	.300	.400	.296	.123	1.34

Name	Class	Cream	1-2-3	$$$$$	Load	Final
Magnificent Lindy	1.83	.500	.375	.273	.119	1.27
Rascal Lass	2.89	.700	.189	.313	.120	1.11
Le L'Argent	2.13	.400	.313	.200	.117	1.11
Lucy Manette	2.50	.650	.238	.185	.118	1.05
Tabayour	1.67	.700	.333	.119	.117	1.03
Wising Up	2.64	.600	.229	.149	.118	1.01
Lady On The Run	1.23	.700	.338	.132	.115	0.90
Foxy Deen	2.54	.600	.162	.115	.119	0.74
Just Anything	1.00	.700	.250	.132	.118	0.68

* Division champion

Bear witness to the most schizophrenic campaign in the history of racing. By all rights, Lady's Secret, a tiny, gray daughter of Secretariat, should have been the hands-down champion of the 3-year-old filly division. She became the first horse to sweep the three major New York races for fillies and mares, the Maskette, Ruffian, and Beldame. She beat all but one opponent, her older stablemate Life's Magic, in the $1,000,000 Breeders' Cup Distaff. She split two decisions with the filly Triple Crown winner, Mom's Command, and handily defeated Fran's Valentine and Kamikaze Rick the only times they met.

So what's this 2.41 rating hanging up there like a wad of dried gum on a phone booth? Shouldn't I hide these ratings in shame and finish the book with dirty limericks?

Well, Lady's Secret actually had two seasons in 1985. Toss out the first one and you've got a champion. Problem is, the whole year counts.

Lady's Secret raced 17 times, winding up with 10 wins and 5 seconds to go with $994,349 in earnings. The racing world really did not take her seriously, however, until her eleventh start of the season, the Test Stakes at Saratoga on August 1. Her 2-length victory over Mom's Command that day set off a flurry of fireworks that did not stop until her second-place finish to Savannah Slew in the La Brea Stakes at Santa Anita on December 27.

Through the first seven months of the year, Lady's Secret won 5 of 10 starts, failed to win in three graded races, and earned $215,249. Had her year ended after beating ordinary allowance mares in the Rose Stakes on July 6 at Belmont, her final rating would have been 1.04. Her performances were steadily improving, but nothing prepared racing fans for the leap to come.

Her "second season" rates considerably higher, especially after five wins in seven starts, all of them graded races, with a class figure of 3.85 (compared to 1.60 in the first half) and earnings of $779,100. Based on those last seven starts, Lady's Secret would have had a 3.94 final rating, well ahead of the division topper and champion, Mom's Command, at 3.01.

Lady's Secret could not hide from her past. Eclipse Award voters were impressed by her second half, but nothing could erase those first seven months when she won only one of four races in California, then popped up here and there to win minor events of no particular significance.

In 1986 Lady's Secret put forth a full-blooded, "January-to-January" season, as her trainer, Wayne Lukas, likes to say. She ran 15 times, won 10 races, all of them graded, and earned $1,871,053. And she won the championship that could have been hers with a better first half in 1985.

OLDER MALES

Name	Class	Cream	1-2-3	$$$$$	Load	Final
*Vanlandingham	5.80	1.175	.360	1.223	.122	3.86
Precisionist	4.33	1.300	.367	1.229	.126	3.42
Greinton	5.92	1.450	.300	.968	.122	3.30
Track Barron	4.00	1.100	.378	.765	.124	2.82
Gate Dancer	5.70	1.100	.180	1.230	.126	2.58
Lord At War	4.50	1.175	.288	.694	.125	2.45
Barberstown	3.00	.700	.450	.564	.119	2.35
Garthorn	2.00	.967	.525	.625	.115	2.30
Imp Society	1.64	1.736	.436	.604	.123	2.20
Dr. Carter	2.50	.933	.375	.596	.120	2.00
Carr De Naskra	4.13	.600	.275	.432	.121	1.85
Bounding Basque	4.38	1.373	.192	.522	.116	1.74
Forzando	3.60	.933	.270	.369	.119	1.71
My Habitony	2.90	.767	.250	.321	.116	1.35
Pine Circle	3.40	.925	.160	.218	.116	1.03
Hail Bold King	3.14	.600	.157	.300	.121	1.01
Wild Again	2.50	.100	.225	.292	.120	1.00
Key To The Moon	2.18	.767	.209	.136	.121	0.87

* Division champion

In no other division are the subtleties of a comprehensive ratings system more vividly illustrated. The Eclipse Award champion, Vanlandingham, comes out .44 ahead of Precisionist, who in turn edged Greinton by .12. In head-to-head competition during the season, Vanlandingham finished ahead of Greinton in both of their encounters, the Marlboro Cup and the Jockey Club Gold Cup. Vanlandingham never faced Precisionist, but Greinton did—six times. They each won three while the other finished second, although Precisionist carried more weight than Greinton on every occasion.

What eventually separated Vanlandingham from Precisionist was the class of his opposition. Racing in the East, where there are more graded races than in California, Vanlandingham had many more opportunities to prove himself against quality fields than did Precisionist, who competed primarily in southern California. Ironically, it was the presence of both Precisionist and Greinton in southern California that discouraged most East Coast horsemen from shipping out West, even though the purses were huge. They knew they would be running for third-place money at best, a daunting proposition.

Greinton, unfortunately, lost a lot more often than he won (3 wins in 12 starts). But his lowly 1-2-3 figure is rescued by his class/cream figure, a resounding 7.37, tops in this division.

Not even a class/cream figure of 6.80 (third best) and a $$$$$ figure of 1.230 (first) could save Gate Dancer from his squalid 1-2-3 figure of .180 (second worst). The greatest skills of trainer Jack Van Berg and jockeys Pat Day, Laffit Pincay, and Chris McCarron managed to squeeze just one lonely little win out of the reluctant Gate Dancer, whose lasting claim to fame will not be his record-setting Preakness of 1984, nor his near-miss in the 1984 and '85 editions of the Breeders' Cup Classic. It will be his trademark earmuffs—the badge of a looney rogue—wiggling down the stretch as he searched desperately for a way to lose another close one.

To be fair, the ratings do give Gate Dancer ample credit for finishing second and third in such rich and famous races as the Marlboro Cup, the Santa Anita Handicap, the Jockey Club Gold Cup, and Charles H. Strub Stakes, all of them rife with top-quality horses. At the other extreme, the ratings reward a horse named Imp Society with a 2.20, even though nobody showed up for any of his dances.

Imp Society was a virtuoso playing alone in the forest for most of the 1985 campaign. From early January to late July he ran in 11 consecutive graded races, won 7 of them, and finished second twice. But, with the exception of the Metropolitan Handicap, he never faced more than one other top-quality opponent in any of those events. Hence, his class rating ended up a measly 1.64, lowest among the 18 older horses rated. He obviously deserved some credit for maintaining such a high performance standard in races that were supposed to attract top company, and that's where his cream rating of 1.736 (highest of those rated) stepped in to balance the scales.

OLDER FEMALES

Name	Class	Cream	1-2-3	$$$$$	Load	Final
Adored	3.00	1.150	.450	.519	.125	2.51
Dontstop Themusic	3.18	1.175	.355	.461	.122	2.13
Heatherten	2.71	.933	.386	.392	.125	1.92
*Life's Magic	4.38	1.454	.185	.649	.120	1.85
Mitterand	2.50	1.175	.350	.400	.120	1.81
Sefa's Beauty	2.17	1.129	.358	.455	.121	1.76
Lovlier Linda	2.75	.986	.288	.397	.121	1.60
Isayso	2.17	.933	.367	.293	.118	1.55
Love Smitten	2.17	.700	.300	.164	.118	1.14
Alabama Nana	1.81	.767	.288	.201	.118	1.06
Sintrillium	2.30	.843	.210	.281	.120	1.06
Flip's Pleasure	1.54	1.100	.215	.237	.118	0.92
Basie	1.79	.700	.250	.174	.117	0.91

* Division champion

The older fillies and mares of 1985 were badly embarrassed by 3-year-old fillies late in the year. Lady's Secret swept the major fall titles in New York, and Videogenic picked up the leftovers in the Ladies Handicap. The result was that precious few older fillies and mares qualified for our study group, as well as a predictably low final rating for the top members of the division.

Adored, Dontstop Themusic, Sefa's Beauty, Heatherten, Mitterand, and champion Life's Magic presented dramatically different types of campaigns. A few points in any direction could have swayed the final ratings dramatically. Adored's season was short and very sweet, ended by injury after only four races, three of them brilliant. Dontstop Themusic began her season slowly, peaked in the summer and early fall, and then failed when all the marbles were on the table and the championship was hers to win. Heatherten had an admirably consistent season, also curtailed by injury; but she was able to dominate a top-class field on only one occasion. Sefa's Beauty won 7 of 12 starts to accumulate the second-highest bankroll of the division; if she hadn't run her two worst races of the year in the Ruffian and Spinster, the title could have been hers. Mitterand was so good so early that no one way paying attention. By the time the summer rolled around she was badly off form and quietly disappeared.

And then there was Life's Magic, who labored anonymously throughout most of the year. She was healthy and hearty, never missing an assignment or a meal. And yet, as the season entered November, she had managed only one win in a dozen starts while finishing out of the money five times. Granted, 4 of those 12 starts had come against males, and Life's Magic came within a half-length of becoming the first filly in 40 years to win the Brooklyn Handicap. But her decent performances against males could not outweigh her failures against her own sex.

Then came the Breeders' Cup Distaff and complete absolution. Life's Magic was in a world of her own that cold November day, winning by more than 6 lengths. As her trainer, Wayne Lukas, said, "She won when she had to."

In terms of her final rating, Life's Magic had the best $$$$$ figure and was way out in front on class and cream figures. She had to be in order to salvage her 1-2-3 figure of .185. The only Eclipse champion in history with a lower winning percentage was Trillion, who was voted female grass champion of 1979 with an 0-for-4 record in North America; but at least Trillion, with four seconds, would have had a .300 figure in her 1-2-3 column.

Eclipse Award voters settled for the one-race campaign of Life's Magic in lieu of the others at the top of the weak division. There was no real help comparing head-to-head records, either. Heatherten actually beat Life's Magic in three of four encounters. Dontstop Themusic and Life's Magic split two matches. At one time or another Sefa's Beauty beat Life's Magic, Heatherten, and Mitterand. Adored never faced the champ at all, which may have worked to the advantage of Life's Magic. Perhaps, in a division so scrambled and disparate, a rating system independent of emotion or perceived superiority is the only way to determine a champion.

TURF—MALES

Name	Class	Cream	1-2-3	$$$$$	Load	Final
Strawberry Road	7.00	.933	.267	1.112	.129	3.36
**Shadeed	5.20	.900	.380	.549	.125	2.99
Sharannpour	6.00	.933	.333	.535	.120	2.96
Teleprompter	4.86	.933	.300	.962	.131	2.83
Win	5.00	.986	.300	.587	.123	2.50
*Cozzene	3.25	1.100	.363	.773	.122	2.48
Yashgan	5.70	1.122	.270	.422	.125	2.39
Tsunami Slew	5.92	1.450	.231	.421	.121	2.24
Both Ends Burning	5.40	1.050	.260	.391	.124	2.19
Al Mamoon	5.25	1.011	.242	.502	.117	2.13
Zoffany	3.18	.650	.391	.513	.118	2.13
Dahar	5.10	1.300	.240	.376	.123	2.03

Name	Class	Cream	1-2-3	$$$$$	Load	Final
Flying Pidgeon	4.92	1.282	.231	.387	.118	1.94
Prince True	3.83	.900	.250	.602	.122	1.91
Drumalis	4.33	.900	.250	.448	.120	1.88
Kings Island	3.13	.900	.313	.477	.116	1.85
**Danger's Hour	2.73	1.425	.318	.390	.119	1.83
Selous Scout	2.78	.900	.333	.452	.116	1.79
**Noble Fighter	3.33	.700	.278	.515	.123	1.76
Cool	3.13	.650	.363	.220	.114	1.71
Jupiter Island	3.88	1.175	.275	.189	.126	1.70
MourJane	4.67	.843	.211	.374	.120	1.56
Bob Back	4.90	1.200	.200	.276	.128	1.62
Nassipour	3.39	1.450	.211	.351	.117	1.49
Late Act	2.89	.933	.300	.215	.121	1.48
Fatih	2.64	.900	.291	.315	.116	1.46
Cariellor	5.00	.986	.200	.130	.128	1.46
Pass The Line	3.45	1.200	.227	.268	.115	1.44
Long Mick	4.43	.700	.229	.142	.121	1.44
**Baillamont	5.50	.986	.175	.138	.124	1.40
Western	2.00	.700	.350	.287	.118	1.35
**Slew The Dragon	1.22	.700	.433	.386	.118	1.33
The Noble Player	3.57	.500	.214	.198	.120	1.11
Majestic Shore	3.00	.650	.217	.241	.119	1.15
Dr. Schwartzman	2.33	.767	.258	.182	.118	1.10
**First Norman	2.89	.843	.211	.174	.116	1.08
Semillero	2.82	.925	.182	.268	.117	1.07
**Charming Duke	1.44	.700	.322	.253	.123	1.07
Stay The Course	1.40	.700	.380	.144	.119	1.06
Jack Slade	3.25	.650	.175	.201	.121	1.01
Ends Well	3.89	.843	.144	.188	.115	0.98
Who's For Dinner	3.58	.767	.158	.161	.118	0.96
**Derby Wish	1.28	.900	.311	.164	.116	0.96
**Don't Say Halo	2.00	.925	.233	.142	.119	0.94
Tri For Size	2.19	.650	.200	.142	.116	0.83
Sondrio	2.64	.400	.173	.144	.117	0.79

* Division Champion
** 3-year-old

The game becomes most susceptible to international influence when it comes to turf competition. Foreign horses raiding major North American turf races are becoming commonplace, and therefore should be treated the same as their Yank counterparts in a ratings analysis. Class figures were based on the frequency of top-quality horses present in all races (European and North American), and cream was, as always, determined by the success and frequency of competition in graded races. (The only difference is that the English, Irish, French, and Italians call graded races "Group" races.) Top-quality European horses were determined by the list of Group race winners abroad, Group 1 seconds and thirds, and horses within 10 pounds of the topweight in the divisions of the widely recognized International Handicap. In 1985, 91 horses qualified under those criteria. Of those, 27 competed in at least one North American event.

Three of the four top-rated male turf horses of 1985 were based in Europe and owned by people in the high-octane economic range. Strawberry Road was campaigned by aerospace millionaire Allen Paulson and renowned art dealer Daniel Wildenstein. Shadeed carrried the colors of Prince Maktoum al Maktoum, a member of the ruling family of Dubai. And Teleprompter belonged to none other than Lord Derby, one of England's cornerstone racing names.

Strawberry Road is without a doubt the most traveled thoroughbred racehorse of the 1980s. As a matter of fact, his 1985 campaign, during which he raced in France, England, and the United States, was relatively conservative by his previous standards. In 1984 he began the season at home in his native Australia where he was a national sports hero. By the summer, he was training in Germany and winning that country's biggest race for older horses. From there it was off to the East Coast of America, and then straight to Los Angeles for the first Breeders' Cup Turf event on November 10, 1984. Shortly after finishing fourth in that $2,000,000 extravaganza, Strawberrry Road was on his way again, headed for Tokyo and a start in the Japan Cup. He split the field of 14, finishing 4 lengths behind the winner in seventh place.

Strawberry Road finally got a rest in his new home in France during the winter and spring of 1985. He needed it. The horses he was to face in 1985 earned him a class figure of 7.00, highest among all 192 names in the study group. Despite winning only two of six starts in France, England, and the United States, Strawberry Road put together the highest rating on a long and highly competitive list.

His 3.36 rating was .37 higher than that of Shadeed and .40 better than Teleprompter's. Shadeed, winner of the first leg of the English Triple Crown, the 2,000 Guineas, ran only once in the United States. He finished fourth in the Breeders' Cup Mile, then was moved up to third place upon the disqualification of the horse who finished second, Palace Music. Like Strawberry Road, Shadeed and Teleprompter bring high class figures into their equations, which would be typical of all top European horses if they were regularly rated. There are fewer Group race opportunities in the major thoroughbred countries of England, France, and Ireland than in North America (346 compared to 401 in 1985). Therefore, the best horses tend to face each other more often.

(Ironically, Teleprompter picked up most of his class points in his two U.S. appearances, the Budweiser Million and Breeders' Cup Turf. As a gelding, he was not allowed to compete in Group 1 races in Europe, an outlandish rule which has since been modified.)

There was no standout North American-based turf horse in 1985, a common perception accurately reflected by the ratings. The top 10 domestics, from Sharannpour through Flying Pidgeon, were separated by just 1.02 rating points, by far the tightest grouping in any division. Knowing this, who can be surprised to find out that there were 19 different winners of the 21 North American Grade I turf races for 3-year-olds and upward in 1985? (The only double winners were Prince True and Selous Scout, and their overall ratings were not good enough to crack the top 10.)

Eclipse Award voters, baffled by the parity, decided to key upon a single race to determine their champion. And so, despite a class/cream figure that was twenty-third on the list of 46 horses and a rating no better than sixth overall, Cozzene was able to sway the vote his way because of his resounding victory in the $1,000,000 Breeders' Cup Mile on national television (the telecast itself had a 4.0 rating and an 11 audience share).

Sharannpour, on the other hand, was buried in his Breeders' Cup race, the $2,000,000 Turf. Such dismal timing effectively erased his good season of three major stakes wins during a bicoastal campaign. Television does more than just elect Presidents.

TURF—FEMALES

Name	Class	Cream	1-2-3	$$$$$	Load	Final
*Pebbles	5.60	1.300	.540	2.444	.128	6.30
Sabin	2.00	1.100	.600	.723	.126	2.71
Estrapade	4.45	1.400	.336	.547	.122	2.63
Fact Finder	4.75	1.450	.225	.407	.119	1.92
Tamarinda	4.17	.400	.300	.262	.120	1.75
Johnica	3.30	.933	.320	.213	.116	1.68
**Devalois	3.29	.933	.300	.291	.121	1.68
Possible Mate	2.70	.650	.340	.288	.120	1.55
Agacerie	3.00	.650	.310	.283	.119	1.53
L'Attrayante	4.08	1.100	.223	.224	.120	1.50
Persian Tiara	4.73	1.454	.173	.224	.118	1.41
Salt Spring	1.75	.767	.125	.219	.115	1.30
Key Dancer	2.86	.767	.271	.190	.118	1.29
Capichi	3.86	.767	.214	.171	.118	1.28
Vers La Caisse	2.30	.300	.330	.228	.116	1.20
Savannah Dancer	2.10	.767	.280	.261	.118	1.18
Lake Country	2.08	.633	.308	.137	.120	1.09

Name	Class	Cream	1-2-3	$$$$$	Load	Final
**Videogenic	1.46	1.100	.277	.173	.115	1.00
Daily Busy	3.17	.633	.167	.197	.117	0.95
**Jolly Saint	2.00	.700	.217	.128	.121	0.83
Eastland	2.75	.767	.150	.153	.117	0.80
**Dawn's Curtsey	1.92	.650	.200	.149	.115	0.78

* Division champion
** 3-year-old

You have just entered the Twilight Zone. This division gives new meaning to the word *arbitrary*. The female turf category was dreamed up in 1979 to answer a question raised by the supporters of Waya, the dominant mare on the grass in 1978: "Hey, how come she didn't get no Eclipse Award?"

Well, the following year Waya crossed up everybody and did enough to win Eclipse Awards in female dirt *and* turf categories. Waya got the more traditional nod for her main track accomplishments, while Trillion (remember 0-for-4 Trillion?) became an embarrassing first winner of the Eclipse Award among fillies and mares specializing in turf racing. With one brilliant stroke, the championships of two divisions—turf and female dirt—were diluted by a third bastard category.

Anyway, in 1985 there was only one turf mare in the world. Her name was Pebbles, and she would have been awarded the male turf award, too, if she could have passed the physical. All five of her races (four in England and one in America) were against predominantly male fields. She won four and finished second in the other. Her victories included one of the richest in Great Britain (the Dubai Champion Stakes) and the richest on grass in the U.S. (the Breeders' Cup Turf).

Pebbles had a rating of more than double the next name on the list, that being Sabin, whose campaign was over before the New Year's Eve party had been cleaned up. Sabin's one and only race took place on January 1, 1985, in the La Prevoyante Handicap at Calder. She won, of course, and went right to the breeding shed.

Sabin's victory should more properly be defined as the climax to her banner 1984 campaign, during which she won 9 of 11 outings and came within one race of a championship. But we are prisoners of the racing calendar, and Sabin gets rated right along with Videogenic, the 3-year-old filly who ran 26 times in 1985.

Females have far fewer opportunities to compete against each other in major turf races than do their male counterparts. There were only 42 graded turf races for females in all of 1985, coast to coast. If they wanted to jump in against the boys there were plenty of chances—80 to be exact.

To maximize the investment in a racehorse, some owners are forced to step out of a traditional division and take a gamble. Such was the case with Estrapade. Her people knew she belonged with females on the turf (and preferably in California, where she could be legally given a diuretic to prevent chronic, stress-related bleeding in the respiratory system). Because of these limitations, Estrapade appeared in a wide variety of contexts: against females on the dirt, against males on the turf, and even against males on the dirt. To more accurately portray her season, her three dirt races were thrown out of her ratings analysis, leaving us with a 3.47 when properly placed. Still no Pebbles, but clearly best of the rest.

SPRINTERS

Name	Class	Cream	1-2-3	$$$$$	Load	Final
*Precisionist	5.33	.700	.200	1.538	.126	2.87
**Smile	5.00	.200	.300	.938	.124	2.62
Fighting Fit	4.00	.650	.300	.400	.125	1.92
**Pancho Villa	3.17	.933	.350	.341	.121	1.90
**Another Reef	1.75	1.100	.475	.402	.119	1.87
Mt. Livermore	2.33	1.233	.373	.364	.122	1.82
Raja's Shark	1.25	1.100	.525	.273	.120	1.63
Charging Falls	2.82	.900	.273	.226	.119	1.36
**Clocks Secret (f)	1.63	.700	.425	.191	.116	1.29
**Phone Trick	1.50	.000	.600	.247	.120	1.27
**Ziggy's Boy	2.36	.633	.318	.186	.117	1.26
Rocky Marriage	1.50	.700	.313	.173	.118	0.98
Debonaire Junior	1.50	.300	.213	.182	.125	0.69

* Division champion
** 3-year-old
(f) Filly

A sprint division award makes a little bit more sense than one for females on the turf, but only a little. Until the 1970s, you could usually count on the sprint champion being the fastest horse running 6 or 7 furlongs under a respectable weight. Then the wheels came off. Nowadays, the sprint champion could be from any of the following mutant groupings:

1. The second-best 3-year-old (usually the one who led the Kentucky Derby into the stretch at short odds and then stopped).

2. A horse with a flashy record, like 9-0 or 10-1. Doesn't matter where they ran up those wins, either. Gives the fastest horse in Pennsylvania or Minnesota a fighting chance.

3. A miler. Only Joan Benoit would consider a mile race to be a

sprint. In Europe there are separate championships for sprinters and milers.

4. A top older horse that doesn't fit anywhere else. The sprint championship becomes a consolation prize, thereby robbing a truly deserving candidate.

There were 10 horses designated "sprinters" from the study group, based on the most comon context in which they competed. Three other names were added—Precisionist, Smile, and Phone Trick—for reasons to be explained shortly. The resulting group comprised a mixed bag of 3-year-olds, a filly, and mainstream older sprinters. The only races considered in rating these sprinters were their sprints, which included events of anywhere from 5 to 7 furlongs.

Pancho Villa and Smile were 3-year-olds who turned in excellent races at a variety of distances. (Smile's nine-race campaign included only three sprints, so he could just as easily have been kept among his contemporaries in the 3-year-old division, where his overall rating of 1.87 placed him tenth behind Spend A Buck.) Fighting Fit and Mt. Livermore were more in the classic sprinter mold, although Fighting Fit ended up with his best payday of the year going 1⅛ miles.

Precisionist, the sprint champion, was a horse whose best distance was 1⅛ miles, who defeated Greinton and Gate Dancer at 1¼ miles, ran a mile in 1:32⅘, and was only 1 for 3 in actual sprints. (As it turns out, those sprints did not hurt his overall rating. Without them Precisionist is still second to Vanlandingham among older horses with a 3.42 rating.) When it came to sprinting, however, Precisionist's timing was . . . precise. In the spirit of Cozzene and Life's Magic, Precisionist chose the right day to sprint like a champ when he defeated Smile, Mt. Livermore, Pancho Villa, and Fighting Fit in the $1,000,000 Breeders' Cup Sprint.

Essentially, the deck is stacked against sprinters. High-profile opportunities are few and far between. Of the 401 graded races in North America in 1986, only 19 of them were sprints open to 3-year-olds and upward of both sexes. Fillies and mares were given only nine opportunities to earn graded credentials in sprints. America, land of the free and home of the swift, badly undervalues its best, brightest, and fastest when it comes to thoroughbred racing.

The most stunning recent example of the sprint division inequity centered on a ball of flame named Phone Trick. As a 3-year-old in 1985, Phone Trick went 6 for 6 at Santa Anita Park and Hollywood Park, carrying an average of 120 pounds while setting two track records and winning two stakes. Not only was he ignored by Eclipse Award voters (he received three votes from the National Turf Writers Association), he was also overlooked by Eual Wyatt, the racing secretary at Garden State Park and the Meadowlands, who compiled the *Daily Racing Form* divisional handicaps. Wyatt rated him at 112 pounds, alongside such world-class unknowns as Felter on the Quay, Vincenne's Road, and Rollin on Over.

(Richard Mandella had the right idea. When informed of Wyatt's slight, the trainer of Phone Trick replied, "I'm heading for New Jersey as soon as possible. Looks like I'll get a break in the weights there for sure.")

The answer? Either elevate more sprint races to graded status, allowing sprinters to develop nationwide reputations, or eliminate such incongruities as the $1,000,000 Breeders' Cup Sprint and the Eclipse Award for the division. Stop exalting them with one hand and slapping them with the other. Talk about mixed messages!

How Far Can We Go?

Can such a ratings system be used to predict the outcome of races—to handicap? Unfortunately, the answer is no, not without some modification to the approach.

Rating horses according to our system is like wide-screen viewing. Handicapping is nothing less than microscopic examination. A highly rated horse may have certain weaknesses in the context of a specific race; the handicapper must still discover and prey upon those weaknesses.

To illustrate the difference between handicapping horses for profit and rating horses for posterity, let's apply the ratings formula to a field of runners as if we were trying to pick a winner. Subject: the 1986 Santa Ynez Stakes at Santa Anita Park, a Grade III race for 3-year-old fillies at a distance of 7 furlongs on the dirt.

Calling upon the same criteria used to rate the upper echelon of 1985 competitors, the field unfolded like this:

Horse	Final Rating	Odds	Finish
Wee Lavaliere	0.78	7.0–1	6th
Sari's Heroine	0.70	2.8–1	1st
Top Corsage	0.54	8.7–1	4th

Horse	Final Rating	Odds	Finish
Firesweeper	0.52	8.6–1	7th
Life at the Top	0.36	4.4–1	3rd
An Empress	0.28	1.8–1	2nd
Tropical Holiday	0.26	38.7–1	5th
Miss Benson	0.20	42.9–1	8th

Rating and handicapping were in agreement on the two hopeless longshots in the field—Miss Benson and Tropical Holiday—as well as the eventual winner, Sari's Heroine. What the ratings did not account for, however, was the recent high regard for An Empress, a filly with a careful, unambitious past, and Life at the Top, whose history was altered by injury.

In order to successfully pick winners with a broad ratings system, more weight must be given to recent races, to trends in the race-by-race changes in the ratings, or to races in the past that come close to the present circumstances. Horses, like all athletes, have good days and bad. The idea behind ratings is to measure the proportion of good to bad; the idea behind handicapping is to decide whether or not *today* will be good or bad.

About Time

The obsession with rating racehorses is a growing industry. English racing fans have their *Timeform*, a year-end volume that assigns hypothetical weights to the best runners of the season and includes a commentary on each horse. There are no mathematical principles at work; *Timeform* is essentially an expanded version of the *Daily Racing Form* Free Handicap. Instead of cold figures dropped in the lap of the racing fan, *Timeform* offers a concise, analytical justification for its weights.

Timeform will soon have an American cousin. Bill Oppenheim, the outspoken editor of the iconoclastic *Racing Update*, and *Washington Post* racing columnist Andrew Beyer are collaborating on a publication that will attempt to rate the year's 1,500 to 2,000 top performers on this side of the Atlantic. Unlike *Timeform*, however, the new project will rely heavily on Beyer's famous "speed figures," which are so popular with handicappers, instead of arbitrary weight assignments.

"I have always been amazed that breeders are willing to make multi-million-dollar investment decisions without, in many cases, any real understanding of a horse's actual level of achievement," Beyer said in announcing the publication. "Breeders often assume, 'This horse won a Grade I race, so he must have delivered a Grade I performance.' This is just not necessarily the case."

Beyer's participation in such a ratings project seems a natural extension of his evolving theories on handicapping. He has moved from the classic school of speed figures to an increasingly observational stance, trusting what he sees as well as what he computes. Rating horses at the end of each season is an old game. Rating them empirically is a new discipline. With the help of handicappers such as Beyer, year-end ratings will not only provide more precise historical perspective but also will give us a leg up on the future—when the betting windows are open.

Old Ways Die Hard

As a practical matter, one should not try to compare horses which never raced against each other, horses which raced in different years, different eras, because conditions affecting racing performance change.

That it is impractical, or unreasonable, or inconclusive to compare a current performer with a memory does not preclude racing men from forming an opinion on the relative merit of race horses, however.

There is a fundamental urge to place greatness in perspective—which is impossible, of course, for there is no fixed standard of greatness in a single era, much less different eras.

Still, smart people who hang around libraries a lot are forever comparing presidents for greatness—academicians who never saw Washington or Jefferson race. And baseball statisticians argue about where to put Ted Williams in the Speaker-Cobb-Ruth all-time outfield, because Williams hit .406. As though greatness could be measured by a number.

—Kent Hollingsworth, *The Blood-Horse*

Racing fans rarely argue about the best horse in a given race on the day's program. They let their money do the talking. But when it comes to the great racehorses of the past, fans never stop beating each other over the head with their personal favorites.

Sometimes these historical arguments have been organized into fascinating experiments. In 1968, when personal computers were the stuff of science fiction, the English wiz kids in the Department of Computational and Statistical Science at the University of Liverpool were handed a peculiar assignment.

Who was the greatest horse of all time?

They whittled from a list of traditional superstars from the twentieth century, using track records, winning percentages, weight carried, and relative earnings to cull the great from the less great. Then, when they had a field of 12, they programmed in running styles and came up with a dream race.

The starting field included Triple Crown winners Citation, War Admiral, and Count Fleet; Horses of the Year Kelso, Native Dancer, Buckpasser, Swaps, Nashua, and Tom Fool; and, from the more distant past, Man o' War, Equipoise, and Exterminator.

Radio station WIOD in Miami took the results, created a call, and dubbed it "The Race of the Century" when it was aired in early April of 1968. The outcome was surprising, controversial, and, ultimately, unsatisfying to aficionados of thoroughbred racing.

Noted racing writer Kent Hollingsworth trotted out some of his best indignation after the broadcast. Preaching from his pulpit as editor of *The Blood-Horse* (first published in 1916), Hollingsworth took both radio station and computer programmers to task:

"Hrumph. Man o' War beaten. Indeed," he wrote.

"One day, shortly after Man o' War was retired to stud, Miss Elizabeth Daingerfield looked out her office window and saw him running in his paddock with the majestic, unrestrained power that was intrinsically his. She called to John Buckner, a wise old stud groom who had handled the fire of Peter Pan when he managed the James R. Keene stallions . . .

" 'Buck! Don't you see him ripping and running in that paddock? Stop him before he gets hurt!'

" 'Why, Miss Lizbeth, iffn all the good horses in New York couldn't ketchim, how'n you expect *me* to stop Man o' War?'

"If legend serves, the task was too great for mere man or beast," Hollingsworth continued. "So a computer was engaged. It was necessary to leave the country to find a machine that could digest figures in such a way to print out a suggestion that Man o' War could be beaten carrying a feathery 126 pounds at a mile and one-quarter.

"No racing man would propose—as did WIOD's call—that Buckpasser could take the track (2 lengths on top after a half mile) from such as Man o' War or, for that matter, War Admiral, Swaps, and Count Fleet. This is as outrageous as suggesting that Babe Ruth would get only singles off Christy Mathewson, that Bill Tilden would move up two steps on Pancho Gonzales' serve.

"For Buckpasser (who ran his best when a stablemate took care of the early speed) and Citation (who usually came from just off the pace) to be knocking heads on the lead from the start, Man o' War had to be facing the other way at the break, Count Fleet had to go to his knees, and little War Admiral had to be knocked sideways. As for Eddie Arcaro having Nashua tenth after a quarter-mile, the name of a substitute rider must have been inadvertently inserted by the computer.

"The machine figured (without an opportunity to assess Colin's unbeaten record, or that of Sysonby, whose sole defeat came when he was drugged by a groom) that Citation could have beaten Man o' War by a neck with Buckpasser third by three-quarters of a length, followed by Exterminator, Kelso, Swaps, Nashua, Tom Fool, War Admiral, Native Dancer, Equipoise, and Count Fleet.

"We figured that if Man o' War were to be beaten again, it might be by Jim Dandy, but, barring that chance, Man o' War would remain the classic shoo-in, Citation a driving second, and an extraordinary dead heat would find 10 horses stretched across the track for show.

"Further, we figured that computer was administered LSD, should have been sent to the spit box, and ruled off the turf."

Come on, Kent, stop pussyfooting. What do you really think?

Sixteen years later, Hollingsworth put his publication on the line and endeavored to come up with a "greatest" list of his own. He used, as his database, the 41 different thoroughbreds who had been voted Horse of the Year from 1936 (when the voting began) through 1982, the year of Conquistador Cielo. To round out the era to an even 50 years, Hollingsworth (through his editorial alter-ego, the crochety Colonel Elsworth) arbitrarily picked three horses as unofficial champions for the years 1933, '34, and '35. Not really scientific, but then it was his ballgame.

He made lists, and more lists, comparing those 44 horses in terms of earnings (with inflation factored in), races won, percentage of races won, and races lost. Then he assembled a composite ranking based on the highest average rankings on the various lists. Hollingsworth came up with the following top 10 from the 1933–1982 half century:

Spectacular Bid
Buckpasser
Native Dancer
Nashua
Affirmed
Citation
Dr. Fager
Round Table
Swaps
War Admiral

Colonel Elsworth did not like the list.

"Well, for one thing, it is a list arrived at by averaging other rankings," he complained. "There is no such thing as average greatness.

"For another, Kelso and Secretariat and Forego did not even make the top 10—which means it has to be a dumb list. . . . Greatness is a matter of opinion, not fact."

So Hollingsworth asked for opinions, inserting a ballot in *The Blood-Horse* of January 14, 1984. Readers were able to list their 10 favorites from the slate of 44 candidates. At that time, *The Blood Horse* had a circulation in the neighborhood of 20,000 copies. There were approximately 2,000 replies.

Ten horses were named on at least half of the ballots. No horse was named unanimously. Many of the 44 were not named at all. But the two at the top would have made it a great race.

Secretariat, the television idol of 1973 who made the covers of *Time, Newsweek,* and *Sports Illustrated* on his way to the Triple Crown, held a slim edge over Kelso, that hard-bodied, high-strung gelding who reigned as America's supreme racehorse from 1960–1964. Secretariat was named on 88.8 percent of the ballots, Kelso on 88.3 percent.

It was a close battle for third place between 1948 Triple Crown winner Citation (with 73.8 percent); the "Gray Ghost," Native Dancer (70.3 percent), whose only loss in 21 starts came in the Kentucky Derby of 1953; and Forego (67.3 percent), the dominant personality of the mid-1970s.

Clustered in the second five were Seattle Slew (58.5 percent), Affirmed (55.3 percent), Spectacular Bid (53.1 percent), Round Table (53.0 percent) and John Henry (50.0 percent).

A historical spot check gives the list some credence. Of course, Secretariat and Kelso never raced against each other. But Secretariat did defeat Forego easily in the 1973 Kentucky Derby. Seattle Slew beat Affirmed both times they met, in the 1978 Marlboro Cup and Jockey Club Gold Cup, while Affirmed narrowly defeated Spectacular Bid in their only encounter, the 1979 Jockey Club Gold Cup. Whether by accident or not, the rankings reflect those results.

More Fans Speak Out

Golden Gate Fields, across the bay from San Francisco, decided to take this "best horse" business into their own hands in the spring of 1986. Using as an excuse their "40 years of racing, 1947–1986," the management staged what they called "The Greatest Race *Never* Run in California."

Golden Gate customers were given the opportunity to pick the winner of a mile and one-quarter main track race among 12 well-known horses that had made at least one appearance in California during the previous four decades. The field was arbitrarily selected by members of the track staff, who, for obvious reasons, included the 1950 handicap star Noor. One of Noor's victories that year was a world-record clocking at a mile and one-quarter in the Golden Gate Handicap.

They left off Kelso, who failed miserably in two California races in 1965; C. V. Whitney's wonderful fillies Bug Brush and Silver Spoon, both victorious over males in major West Coat races; and turf champion Cougar II, who practically owned the grass courses at Santa Anita and Hollywood Park in the early 1970s.

Because of California's major league racing, however, most of the stars of the era were candidates for the local list. Seattle Slew was included, even though he lost the first race of his life in the 1977 Swaps Stakes at Hollywood Park and never came west again. Dr. Fager made just one appearance in California, but it burned in the mind forever. In the 1968 Californian Stakes at Hollywood Park, "The Doctor" carried 130 pounds and won in a waltz, beating champion mare Gamely in the process. Affirmed, Spectacular Bid, Buckpasser, John Henry, Citation, Swaps, and Round Table all were considered national personalities, yet their combined California records show 69 wins in 103 starts and a collective in-the-money rate of 91 percent.

The selection committee also came up with a couple of token entries. Native Diver, the wild-eyed black gelding who was bred in California, earned a million dollars while never winning outside the state. Majestic Prince began his career in the Bay Area and was unbeaten in California before going on to win the 1969 Kentucky Derby and Preakness Stakes.

The fans had a great time. Pure opinion poll. Don't confuse me with facts, they figured. This one is straight from the heart. A total of 7,841 ballots were submitted, then the tally was handed to track announcer John Gibson, who had the job of turning this flight of fancy into a flesh-and-blood race call. Gibson locked himself in his room, spread out the past performances of the 12 horses, and came up with "The Greatest Race *Never* Run."

The first half of the race went pretty much according to historical expectations. Two of the fastest thoroughbreds ever—Native Diver and Dr. Fager—were pressured on the early pace by Seattle Slew. Swaps, the holder of three world records upon retirement, must have napped in the gate. Gibson had him nowhere near the leading group.

Anyway, the pace was too fast to worry about the horses in front sticking around for the finish picture. Would you believe the first 6 furlongs were run in 1:07⅖, within a whisper of the world's record! As Native Diver and Dr. Fager retreated, Seattle Slew, Spectacular Bid, and John Henry began to attack.

"They're in deep stretch!" Gibson was growling like an excited lion. "And it's Seattle Slew in front by a head, John Henry on the outside, and Spectacular Bid. They're head-and-head . . . John Henry now on the outside. It's John Henry taking command—in front!"

If you can believe it, John Henry beat this bunch like they were nailed to the ground, by no less than 3 lengths, while Seattle Slew nosed out Spectacular Bid for second. Citation was fourth and Affirmed was fifth. Affirmed fifth! Hrumph! In his entire career of 29 starts, Affirmed was fifth only once, and on that day his saddle slipped so far up his neck that jockey Steve Cauthen was lucky to stay aboard. Never mind that Spectacular Bid was a perfect 5 for 5 in mile-and-one-quarter races, or that Seattle Slew was caught only *once* after taking the lead in the stretch (and gave away 14 pounds when it happened).

The results are easy to explain, however. In 1984, at the remarkable age of 9, John Henry made his first and only appearance at Golden Gate Fields. The old battler calmly set a turf course record while winning the Golden Gate Handicap. It was an indelible performance, mention of which still raises goose bumps in San Francisco racing circles.

So try to understand why they voted as they did, and forgive them. Here is the count:

John Henry	2,372
Seattle Slew	828
Spectacular Bid	821
Citation	792
Affirmed	647
Noor	570
Swaps	395
Native Diver	316
Dr. Fager	294
Buckpasser	270
Round Table	268
Majestic Prince	268

What a surprise. In a popularity contest, the most popular horse won!

2

A Smile on Every Face, A Winner in Each Race: Handicapping

As a dynamic entity, a horse race will always remain a test of our abilities in pattern recognition, psychology, and money management. Success depends upon passing the test and solving the puzzle correctly. There should be little doubt that attempting such a solution on a continual basis is an intellectual challenge of the highest order.

—Dr. Steven A. Roman, The Thoroughbred Record

There are no immutable truths, no absolute rights and wrongs, because the only meaningful measure of any handicapping method is profitability."

—Andrew Beyer, The Winning Horseplayer

The horses I follow follow horses.

—Anonymous

There is a lot on the line in the game of handicapping horses. Of the $8,254,612,623 bet on thoroughbreds in North America in 1985, approximately 80 percent went back into the pockets of the people who placed the bets. The remaining 20 percent went to taxes (for the privilege of betting legally), to the racetracks (to provide a clean and comfortable environment), and to the people who own, train, ride, and breed the horses (to keep us in more horses).

Thoroughbred racing was designed as a participation sport, of sorts, for the fan. If a fan can't feel the thrill of riding the animals at speeds upward of 40 miles per hour, then the next best thing is being able to watch them perform, while at the same time holding a tangible interest in their success. Nothing creates fan loyalty like a few dollars at risk.

Handicapping horses can take hours or minutes. The decision, once reached, is instantly resolved. It is clean, cut, and dried. No shades of gray at the end of the day. You're either a winner or a loser.

Getting there, however, is always a curious journey. Handicapping sends the racing fan through a maze of numbers, names, and dates, with blind luck always along for the ride. No other sport provides so much information and opinion toward a single goal.

This chapter will attempt to sort out some of the many choices confronting the handicapper as he digs into a day of racing. There are betting systems, which leave very little room for creative thought; and there are handicapping theories, which require a good deal of study and discipline. There are public handicappers to follow, providing the equivalent of "fast food" for picking horses. And then there are dozens of off-the-wall ideas on what makes one horse run faster than another. At the end of the chapter you will be ready to take on the racing game with new energy and insights . . . or you may want to go back to sticking a pin through a program and betting the horses with holes.

The Basics

Don't even touch your wallet until you understand the language. There are certain terms in handicapping that will be flung about here as if everyone were born knowing what they meant. They include:

Speed. The time it takes a horse to run a race. Bet you figured that one out. But there are so many horses, running in so many races under so many different conditions, that "speed" must be redefined constantly. A runner considered a speed demon at one track may run like a plow horse at another.

Track variants. These relate directly to speed and the determination of "how fast is fast?" No two racetracks are identical in terms of soil, bounce, grading, or angles. And no single racetrack is ever the same from day to day because of changes in maintenance and weather. The individual handicapper decides just how much importance these variations deserve.

Pace. The internal character of a race as measured by the times of the horse on the lead. The early pace usually is broken down in quarter-mile increments, while the last part of a race can be interpreted by "eighths." Pace—fast or slow—can compromise some horses while aiding others.

Trouble. Sounds obvious, but the term covers an acre of ground. A horse can have a good effort nullified by any number of tiny roadblocks during a rough-and-tumble race, losing a length here, a half-length there until he is a well-beaten creature. The handicapper must know how much should be excused because of trouble, and how much of the trouble should be blamed on the horse itself.

Class. At a fairly early stage of its career, a horse will reveal just how good or bad he will be the rest of his racing life. And there he usually will stay, running against his own kind. Movement up and down the class ladder triggers alarms and attention. The handicapper needs to find out if the move is logical, or only a pipe dream on the part of a trainer or owner. By the same token, the handicapper must avoid pigeonholing a horse at a particular level too soon or too late. Both can be expensive mistakes.

We Need a Guide

Handicapping can be a pleasure, a profession, or an obsession. Jeff Siegel, a syndicated handicapper for several southern California newspapers, embodies all three.

From time to time in this chapter, Siegel will be our man on the inside, helping us to sort through the challenge of handicapping. He has been in the trenches with the fans and in the Turf Club with the high-rollers. He knows what it's like to bet his last five dollars, or ride along on the crest of an unbelievable winning streak. And yet he has never lost sight of the fan in the grandstand trying to find one lonely little winner to make the day a success.

Siegel is at the track at dawn, stopwatch in hand, clocking horses as they go through their morning drills. He talks with trainers, owners, stable help, and fellow handicappers, picking brains and gathering information. He is at the races every afternoon, watching each event, then watching it again and again on videotape replay, searching for hidden meaning in every horse's move. At home, he is a voracious reader of handicapping theorists such as Tom Ainslie, Andrew Beyer, and anyone else whose experience may offer a new twist on old ideas.

"I remember getting upset when Swaps lost his match race with Nashua," Siegel said one afternoon at Del Mar. "I know that was 1955 and so I know I was 4 years old. Obviously, I've always had an interest in the sport."

Siegel is the perfect guide for a tour through the strange land of handicapping, starting with a few basic lessons for beginners who need a push, and veterans who may need a refresher.

All Systems Go?

The lowest level on the evolutionary scale of handicapping is populated by betting systems. They provide a quick fix for the headaches of lengthy analysis. They also supply a scapegoat in the event of failure. It was, after all, the system that came up with the horse, not the person who played the system.

"Stay away from systems," warns Jeff Siegel, and just about every other handicapping theorist worth his bankroll. "Systems are the biggest ripoff. There is no such thing as a system that can work in the long run. Systems are post facto [after the fact], otherwise they wouldn't work.

"I can make you the greatest post facto system of all time," Siegel adds. "My brother, a math wiz, can input every past performance chart for an entire year in his computer and find out exactly what worked to win races. But don't expect that system to work the following year, because you will have a whole new set of numbers."

Aw c'mon, Jeff. Can't we try just a few systems, just for laughs? Be-sides, betting systems have existed for centuries. The first one probably was hatched when a horse shocked a small crowd gathered on an English heath with a sudden reversal of form. Explanations were necessary to keep the local sheriff from arresting the lot. And so was born the post-facto system of predicting what will happen in a horse race, based upon all the times the same thing happened before.

In his 1955 volume *Making Money at the Races*, New York handicapper David Barr endorsed 36 different betting systems. It was a cookbook for horse players, a "Joy of Gambling" for the racetrack.

Barr presented his systems under such tantalyzing titles as Playing Five-Year-Olds, Beating 'Em in the Bushes, Super-Fine Bests, Class Drop Method, Progressive Place Betting, Get 'Em While They're Hot, Short and Sweet, The Overlay Way, and Trainer's Cover-Up.

"Some people like to use methodical handicapping procedures," Barr wrote, "while others are interested purely in the time factor. Rate them or weight them, the fundamental principles are what count. Get into the swing of things by sticking to a strict set of rules. This way you are sure of betting right, leaving no room for guess work. . . . Things are apt to be a little difficult at the beginning, but when you get the hang of the method you are playing, selections will roll off smooth as butter.''

Of course, almost everyone uses margarine these days. Chances are that many of the ingredients in Barr's methods have become similarly dated. But there may be a few gems applicable even today.

One of the most intriguing of Barr's three dozen systems was The Triple Threat, which considered only claiming races populated by male horses over the age of 2. A horse had to qualify by clinging to three progressively narrowing statistical ledges:

1. Single Threat—Must have run within 10 days of today's race and lost, but not by more than 12 lengths.

2. Double Threat—Must have won for a claiming price in excess of claiming price of today's race.

3. Triple Threat—Must be a switch in jockeys from most recent race, or today's jockey must have won with horse before (according to past performances).

Barr was using some fairly standard methods for handicapping cheap horses, keying on their ability to occasionally resurrect the spirit of past glories, their inconsistency, and their sudden and final loss of form. To this he added the jockey factor. He wanted a rider who had successfully coped with a particular horse's eccentricities before, or a brand new jockey who perhaps would bring fresh inspiration to a reluctant old battler.

Barr conducted a two-month test of The Triple Threat during March and April of 1949, drawing from the race meetings in Florida, New York, Maryland, Louisiana, Arkansas, and California. The system came up with 164 selections, of which 31.7 percent (52 horses) won and 58 percent finished first, second, or third. A standard bet of $2 to win, place, and show on each of the 164 horses showed a net profit of $406.90, or a return of 41.3 percent on a $984 investment. Of the 52 winners, 17 (32.6 percent) returned $10 or more. Barr was quite proud of a horse named Invitation, which popped up as a Triple Threat horse at Old Jamaica racetrack in New York on April 6. Invitation paid $73 to win.

I was curious. Could Barr's Triple Threat work in today's racing world? Could it even be applied? I at least had to give it a spin around the block.

A race at Del Mar in August of 1986 fit the requirements. It was a $10,000 claiming race for 3-year-olds and up, and all of the entrants were males. The vital statistics follow:

Horse	Last Race	Finish	Jockey
Inverness Gaol	Aug. 7	9th	Cisneros
Bob's Intent	July 11	3rd	Pedroza
He's No Mistress	Aug. 4	11th	Lipham
Melchip	Dec. 21	11th	Kaenel
Crimaurie	Aug. 10	3rd	Patterson
Eruptive	July 29	1st	Ortiz
The Big One	July 25	5th	Olivares
Luckalot	Aug. 10	1st	Castanon
Mr. Bar Able	Aug. 10	4th	Sibille
Fray Reflejo	Aug. 10	2nd	Ortega
Apprehend	June 22	6th	Black

The "Single Threat" stage eliminated all but Crimaurie, Mr. Bar Able, and Fray Reflejo. Those three raced within 10 days of the event in question. So did Luckalot, but because he won the race, he is removed from consideration.

The "Double Threat" stage failed to thin the choices any further. All three horses had won for a higher claiming price (or a higher class of race) among those displayed in their *Daily Racing Form* past performances.

The "Triple Threat" stage eliminated Crimaurie. He was to be ridden by Alan Patterson, who had ridden him in his August 10 race. Patterson had never won aboard Crimaurie in the past. Mr. Bar Able, however, qualified on the first count—Ray Sibille was taking over for Jack Kaenel. Fray Reflejo satisfied the alternate jockey requirement: Luis Ortega rode him in the August 10 event, but Ortega also was aboard when Fray Reflejo won a $12,500 claiming event nearly a year before.

When the Triple Threat system provides two choices, Barr recommends the handicapper head for the snack stand and watch the race at arm's length. Just as well. In this particular case, Fray Reflejo finished eighth and Mr. Bar Able was ninth.

Let's go through the Triple Threat on a claiming race run at Belmont Park on June 26, 1985:

Horse	Last Race	Finish	Jockey
Fibak	June 7	3rd	Guerra
Bright Rex	June 16	4th	Velasquez
Colonel Law	May 15	1st	Vasquez
Strike a Coin	June 10	1st	Migliore
Fingers In the Till	June 16	2nd	MacBeth
Hillside View	June 14	6th	Moore

Horse	Last Race	Finish	Jockey
Wandering Feet	June 20	9th	Santagata
Will's First	June20	5th	Davis
See for Free	June 7	4th	Bailey
Account Receivable	May 27	4th	Cordero
Arabian Gift	June 5	1st	Samyn

The survivors of the first cut were Bright Rex, Fingers In the Till, Wandering Feet, and Will's First. Of those, only Will's First had a recent victory at a higher claiming price showing on his published past performances. But did Will's First pass the final test? He did, because Robbie Davis was taking over in the saddle for Nick Santagata. Will's First qualified as a Triple Threat bet, and followers of the system got 14–1 odds. They also got a run for their money. Will's First led the race deep into the stretch before being passed by three horses to be beaten by less than 4 lengths.

Old Time Religion

R. W. Wood, an English gambler, attempted to cover all the bases with his 1950 volume entitled *100 World-Famous Racing Systems*. Chances are only a few of the well-worn methods would pass muster with the modern pari-mutuel information managers. But they are the direct ancestors of today's systems and maybe, just maybe, there is a nugget of insight in there somewhere. Here is a sampling:

"System No. 10 . . . From the day's programme select a 6-furlong event. If more than one, choose the most valuable. If no 6-furlong event, take the nearest above 6 furlongs. Select two horses daily; use one as your "if absent." The selection is the latest winner last time out, providing it has not missed any engagements since winning. If no winner last time out, turn to seconds; and if no seconds, to thirds. If nothing discovered, pass over the day's racing."

The philosophy here being that sprinters tend to stay in form over a greater span of races than do distance horses. There are modern handicapping theorists who agree. Many others, however, will argue just the opposite: Because of its intensity, a sprint is more demanding than a route race and more difficult to recover from physically.

Applying this sytem to the races at Hollywood Park during the week of June 25–29, 1986, we would have been in action every day. The five horses selected by the system were Antique Lace (she finished last at 9–1), American Legion (a winner, paying $4.00), La Preciosa (sixth at 74–1), Lincoln Park (second as the 7–5 favorite), and Precious Bambino (second at 6–1).

Such a system (and its modern derivatives) promotes tunnel-vision at its worst. It proclaims, "If the horse did it before, he can do it again." Even the most common variables—such as class jump, post position, and running style—are ignored. It is impossible for the complete handicapper to accept such a philosophy, which treats the thoroughbred as a machine, able to reproduce winning races no matter what the circumstances.

The successful handicapper never expects so much from a horse. If its best race (on paper) is not good enough to win the specific race in question, then the smart handicapper will wait for another day.

Here's another example of Wood's wisdom:
"System No. 16 . . . Back the horse carrying the most weight of those placed last time out this year, but which is receiving not less than 5 lbs. from the top weight; but if only one horse is so placed, 3 lbs. qualifies. There must be at least three runners, and when more than three of them were placed as above, NO BET. Where three horses were placed last time out this year, all receiving at least 3 lbs. from the top weight, choose the highest weight, unless two placed horses carry the same weight, then it is NO BET; but if only two horses are place horses and both carry the same weight, back the one best placed last time. Equally placed, that is, both seconds or both thirds, NO BET."

This one was included to prove that even the English have trouble with plain English. The system is easy enough to test. All you need is an ordinary handicap race and a sense of humor. The feature race at Belmont Park on a September day in 1985 was a likely candidate. Here are the particulars required:

Horse	Weight	Last Finish
Waitlist	118	1st
Silver Ghost	108	1st
Exattic	119	1st
Diamada	109	8th
Rambling Rector	111	4th
Spender	112	2nd

Eliminate Diamada and Rambling Rector, both out of the money in their last starts. Ignore Exattic. He is the race topweight, against whom the others will be judged. And take out Waitlist. His weight is too close to that of the topweight.

That leaves two viable candidates, according to this system, and the one we must go with is Spender, with 112 pounds, compared to Silver Ghost, with 108. Spender is the bet. Waitlist won the race; Silver Ghost finished second, and Spender was fifth.

In allowing weight to play this important a role in evaluating horses, the handicapper puts himself at the mercy of the track's racing secretary. Whether they are assigned by formula or opinion, weights are rarely a good judge of a horse's ability except after the fact, and even then the connection is usually inconclusive.

A dramatic example of how weights can be misleading involved a major invitational handicap in the early 1980s. The racing secretary neglected to invite a horse who was, by all reasonable standards, an obvious candidate for the event. To issue a late invitation with the proper highweight would have been embarrassing to the racing secretary. So instead, to save face, he included the horse without fanfare, at a lower weight, hoping to hide the mistake. As it turned out, the horse would have no part of it, and subsequently carried his feathery load to an impressive victory.

"System No. 21 . . . This system consists of backing the first and second favourite in every race. Occasionally the two first favourites start at the same price, and in this case the stake is divided on the two horses. The same thing applies when there are two joint second favourites.

"Each horse should be backed with a level stake, but after a losing week, the stakes for the following week should be increased by one quarter, coming back to the original stakes when a profit is shown."

This one caught my interest, probably because I was schooled at the races by my grandmother to throw out the favorite and try to find a reason for betting the second choice. There is a good chance that a favorite will be "underlayed," that is, be a much lower price than the facts and figures logically dictate. If that is the case, then the second choice in the betting could be an "overlay," offering higher odds than expected.

Second choices, of course, do not win as often as favorites win. That is probably why this system hedges a bit and requires its followers to play both favorites and second choices. Okay. I'm game. I took my imagination and my funny money to Gulfstream Park near Miami for a week in February of 1985 and played the first and second choices every day.

We hit a lucky week. Of the 61 races run, 24 of them were won by favorites (39.3 percent) and 15 were won by second choices (24.6 percent). The payoffs ranged from a high of $11.20 to a low of $2.80. The total investment was $246 ($4 per race; $6 on one race with co-favorites) and the total return was $253.40, for a neat profit of $7.40. I wouldn't tell you I was sold on the system, but it's the kind I might try again.

"System No. 41 . . . The system comprises one rule only. In each rule choose the horse that was placed second last time out, and is running over the same distance as the race in which it was placed second. If two or more horses in the same race, give preference to the one that finished nearest the winner. If still unable to divide, support the one carrying the heaviest weight."

Ah, that life were so simple. Those who live by one rule only usually end up breaking a lot of rules. But believe it or not, there are systems alive and selling well today that boil a race down to a single variable.

This system needs a high-powered public relations firm to fly. Chances are it may have worked for a few weeks, or months, or even a year. More likely, it will always work like it did for my imaginary bankroll during a week in May of 1986 at Golden Gate Fields, the track on the eastern shore of San Francisco Bay.

The system gave me 22 horses to bet during that week. Their average odds were nearly 5–1. Their average finish was next to nowhere. Only three of the 22 horses won, all three of them favorites paying $6.40, $6.60, and $4.20. There were also four seconds and four thirds, but that was small consolation unless the betting was done across the board (win, place, and show).

This is probably a typical result for most such single-minded systems. Part of the lure of handicapping thoroughbreds is the complexity of the challenge. If you want simplicity, go spin a wheel.

"System No. 62 . . . When a horse has run ten times without winning, and is still in the same stable, follow it with a small stake each time it runs. If there are more than one in a race, back the lot, as the prices are always big. Thus, you can afford to follow each and increase slightly after each failure, as you missed them during their long run of ten losing races. Refer back to previous year's running to get the ten consecutive losing runs."

Does the phrase "good money after bad" come to mind? The quest for the longshot winner is a noble one, heartily endorsed by your author. There's no better feeling at the racetrack than being right when practically everybody else was wrong. Longshot betting requires a peculiar kind of insight, however. The poor performances of a longshot must be justified by extenuating circumstances, sometimes so subtle that they defy observation by the masses.

Longshot players usually follow individual horses, waiting for the right moment to pounce. This system, on the other hand, blindly follows a proven loser until either lightning strikes or the money runs out. There has never been any justification for the statement, "Well, the horse was bound to win sooner or later."

The system would not have been presented as a system, no matter how arcane, unless it had some success. No doubt there are modern descendants of good ol' No. 62 around today. Longshot systems are like the fellow selling shoes for $500,000. He's not getting much business, but he only needs to sell one pair.

On July 17 at Hollywood Park, three horses fit the "10 loss" system. Two of them were maidens, the other was an older filly. Backing them on this particular day gave us two third-place finishes and a dismal twelfth, all at odds of 12–1 or higher. After that, the three horses went their separate ways.

Maiden No. 1 ran at Hollywood Park five days later and finished third again at odds of 3½–1. On August 16 at Del Mar, he finished second as the 2–1 favorite. On August 29 at Del Mar, he finally won and paid $8.80. If we had bet in progressions of $2, $4, $6, and $8, we would have invested a total of $20 by the time we cashed a $35.20 ticket on the day he won.

Maiden No. 2 headed south of the border to Agua Caliente in Tijuana and ran there August 10, finishing third at 3½–1. Again, at Caliente, on August 24, he finished ninth as the odds-on favorite. One month later at the L.A. County Fair, Maiden No. 2 won and paid $10.60, hardly the windfall we deserved for all that mileage. Nevertheless, with the same $2, $4, $6, $8 progression, the investment was $20 and the winning ticket was worth $31.80.

The older filly was a test of will. In her next five races after our initial encounter, she finished fourth, sixth, sixth, sixth, and fifth at average odds of 17–1. On December 29 at Santa Anita, she turned up in the second race, at odds of almost 15–1. She finished sixth, again. My total investment, based upon the progressions used earlier, would have swollen to $56. I decided to cut my losses and get off the band-wagon, but at the same time I made my friends swear a blood oath to keep the news to themselves if this filly should ever win a race.

Caveat Bettor

For the trusting fan who doesn't mind being led by the nose, most major metropolitan daily newspapers in cities with thoroughbred racing offer "selections" on each day's racing card. So do the several editions of the *Daily Racing Form* and even the newswire services. These selections come in a variety of forms and, more importantly, they come from a variety of handicapping personalities.

The "public handicapper," as the individual is called, could be one of any of the following:

1. A sophisticated, well-rounded student of thoroughbred racing with indepth knowledge, handicapping discipline, and insights worth backing at the betting window.

2. A racing writer who doubles as handicapper, perhaps not as interested in the nuts and bolts of every race but still knowledgeable enough to offer intelligent selections.

3. A member of the sports department who dabbles in handicapping on the side and has talked the sports editor into giving him a chance to do selections.

4. A syndicated handicapper who sells his selections to a variety of publications (sometimes under a variety of names).

Since the newspaper handicapper is the one most frequently read by the general racing public, it pays to find out about the person behind those selections. Newspapers are morally (though not legally) obligated to be open and aboveboard about racing selections just as they are obligated to label the odds and point spreads on football and basketball games. If you want to know who is making the daily selections under the pseudonym "Night Eyes," call up the paper and ask them.

On the other hand, the only true test of a public handicapper is the bottom line—picking winners. Newspapers never hesitate to blow the bugle loud and long when "So-And-So Picks Nine Winners at Yahoo Downs." Nobody hears about the downside, although the New York Racing Association tried to enlighten the public in 1985 by reprinting "standings" of the local public handicappers as published in the Spanish language newspaper, *Noticias del Mundo*. Not surprisingly, the handicapper for *Noticias del Mundo* was at the top of the list at the time. Amid protests from the other public handicappers, the feature was removed from the NYRA program. The fans were back to finding things out for themselves.

It is easy enough to do. And here is a test to illustrate. Let's look at the performance of six public handicappers from around the country—two from a track in each of three major racing centers—and see how they did over a two-week period in early June of 1985. We'll give them each an imaginary bankroll to make a $2 win bet on each of their selections. Then, just to give the test a little twist, we'll also bet $2 on the favorite in every race. The results:

REGION I

Selections	Races	Wins	Profit/Loss	High	Average
Handicapper A	92	24	−$26.60	$14.40	$6.60
Handicapper B	92	17	−$100.60	$ 9.80	$4.80
Favorites	92	28	−$56.60	$ 6.80	$4.40

REGION II

Selections	Races	Wins	Profit/Loss	High	Average
Handicapper C	99	24	−$66.60	$13.00	$5.40
Handicapper D	99	21	−$96.60	$13.00	$4.80
Favorites	99	34	−$36.60	$ 7.20	$4.60

REGION III

Selections	Races	Wins	Profit/Loss	High	Average
Handicapper E	97	32	−$13.80	$18.20	$5.60
Handicapper F	97	26	−$43	$12.00	$5.80
Favorites	97	37	+$ 0.60	$ 9.20	$5.20

No public handicapper would back all of his own selections at the betting window. Even the hard-core gamblers among them pass up the occasional race. But they do have to make a selection in every race, or leave an embarrassing blank in the newspaper column.

It is hard to draw conclusions from only two weeks' worth of data. A public handicapper ideally should be judged on the basis of an entire race meeting, through good and bad weather and a variety of track biases. But at least this cursory look will give you some idea of the wide range of success that public handicappers can have, and how they fare against those who blindly follow each and every favorite.

One note of warning before selling your soul to betting all favorites: The average winning percentage of favorites is widely accepted to be about 33 percent, close to the figure represented by the sample in Region II. Region III experienced an inordinately high percentage of successful favorites during this small time period, while Region I was running slightly behind the norm.

The beginning handicapper usually will go through the rudimentary mechanics of speed, class, distance, weight, and recent form considerations . . . and then arrive at the favorite 9 times out of 10. So why not save time and just wait until the public decides on its betting choice, and then plunge right in with the herd?

Playing only the favorites can be a frustrating, unsatisfying game. Bet them all and you'll win one out of every three races, but that one must pay at least $6.00 (2–1 odds) to make up for the money lost on the other two. Like the man who was scolding a beginner for betting on a horse that was 3–5 said, "If you've got the 'three' you don't need the 'five'."

In the Beginning

Jeff Siegel and other handicapping generalists are the direct descendants of Roi Tolleson, the man who made public touting respectable. They live by one basic rule: "Nothing comes easy at the racetrack."

Tolleson, better known to the subscribers of his famous *Daily Running Horse* as El Rio Rey, was a native of Texas who transplanted himself to New York for the specific purpose of following the ponies. Toney Betts, in *Across the Board*, his 1956 homage to racing's early gamblers, called Tolleson "a horse player's horse player."

"Tolleson revolutionized racing publications," wrote Betts. "He was the first to give the readers speed ratings, easy-to-see and finely detailed past performances, and even such a small but big items as the alphabetical index to the horses running that day.

"His method of handicapping was simple: "Start out by eliminating the losers if you want the winner." He would X-out horses he thought had no chance, boiling the race down to the contenders. The past performances were graded according to his selections, and there appeared, for a time, a line in capital letters: 'It is highly improbable the following horses will be in the money.'"

Information, Please

On the day of the 1986 Kentucky Derby, the Los Angeles edition of the *Daily Racing Form* carried more than two dozen display ads for a variety of handicapping theories, computer ratings, handicapping seminars, money management techniques, and clocker's reports. In June of 1986 the bookshop in the Belmont Park clubhouse was offering more than 20 titles on handicapping theory, most of them published since 1980. Names like Beyer, Ainslie, and Quirin were displayed as if they were Mailer, Sheldon, or Updike.

The handicappers behind these theories assume that the interested fan is willing to spend a little time thinking through the many pieces of information presented by a single race. They are not usually public handicappers in the sense that they issue a set of selections on a daily basis. Rather, they are published authors who constantly refine their ideas and reflect upon their consequences. They are also usually obsessive personalities.

"There's no way that I would wish upon anybody what I'm doing in terms of time and research," and Jeff Siegel in considering his own obsession. "I happen to like what I'm doing. But for every one person like me, there are 10 people who would go off a cliff trying to do the same thing."

So what does he recommend?

"Well, if a person wants to get into handicapping a little bit deeper, without getting terribly serious, I would suggest they try to learn speed methods and pace methods. There are several books on the market that would give a person an appreciation of when a horse is good and when he isn't good when he may appear to be."

And how do we know which theorist to believe?

"As far as handicapping methods are concerned," Siegel noted, "the backbone should be an evaluation of the individual horse. Then all other factors that affect the horse's performance can be taken in."

Handicappers such as Siegel once were considered second-class citizens compared to the statistically oriented theorists who embraced "speed figures," the interrelated numbers assigned horses based on final times.

Yet the disciples of speed figures have a relatively brief lineage. Their gurus blossomed in the 1970s when the superstars of the genre were the larger-than-life *Washington Post* columnist Andrew Beyer, who wrote *Picking Winners*, and the scholarly Dr. William Quirin, author of the computer-oriented and heavily tabled *Winning at the Races*. Both volumes were bestsellers by handicapping standards.

"You cannot be enslaved by a figure," warns Siegel. "I've had enough experience to know when a number is a good number and when it's a phony.

"Occasionally, I will find races that are out of whack. A horse won a $40,000 claiming race in 1:09. Given her average expected final time, other horses should have been running in 1:08 over that same track—but they didn't. So I had to ask myself, 'What caused this freak of nature?' This is where experience comes in. Sometimes a speed horse allowed to run alone on the lead will outdo himself. Maybe there is a malfunction of the timer. I need to find an answer for my own peace of mind. But the important thing is to not bet blindly on that horse the next time, because the figure does not reflect reality."

Apparently the speed-figure boys agreed. As they turned the corner into the 1980s, both Beyer and Quirin expanded their approaches to include a factor referred to simply as "the trip." From out of the swirling hieroglyphics of speed tables and track variants came the revelation that a horse was influenced by more than just the texture of the earth and the speed of his own four legs. Observation became the most valuable tool of the serious handicapper. Subjective analysis of the effects of pace and trip replaced the objective reading of cold, hard speed figures. How a horse got there became more important than when, and, as a result, old dogs learned new tricks.

"I paid a year's tuition for my self-education," Beyer wrote in his 1983 work, *The Winning Horseplayer*. "Learning to watch races perceptively was not easy for me. And when I tried to reconcile my visual observations with my speed figures, I was often hopelessly confused. I lost the clear, simple vision of the game that the figures gave me . . ."

Quirin kept the bandwagon rolling with *Thoroughbred Handicapping—State of the Art*, also published in 1983. In his introduction to the book, Quirin took credit for ringing in the age of scientific handicapping. "However," he wrote, "despite the reputation *Winning at the Races* may have won for me, both as a speed handicapper and a proponent of the scientific approach, I have always placed the major emphasis in my own handicapping on the interpretive side of the game."

James Quinn is among the new wave of handicapping scholars who defy the archaic image of the track tout. No more seedy types with colorful names like Ratbreath, Pockets, and Kid Tomorrow. Quinn is a creature of the 1980s, when every upper-middle-class household comes equipped with a personal computer. The title of his most recent book, *High-Tech Handicapping in the Information Age*, says it all: The fun's over. Making money at the races is serious business, to be approached in the same thoughtful manner as applying for a home loan or choosing the right savings plan.

Quinn advocates greater information access and management, and the use of computers to process and retrieve the growing wealth of information available to horseplayers. His greatest peeve is the narrow-minded handicapper who cannot see beyond his own betting system.

"Handicappers tend to be egocentric," Quinn wrote. "Perhaps that explains why the most common reaction to new or unfamiliar information among practiced handicappers has been to filter it through existing perceptions, beliefs and practices. If the new material fits comfortably enough, it might be used; if not, throw it out. The more things change, the more they remain the same."

Quinn's primary contribution to the nuts and bolts of handicapping is an emphasis upon foreign race records. Such knowledge has become invaluable, especially in the major racing centers where European and South American horses have invaded like locusts. The strong U.S. dollar of the early 1980s sent trainers and agents scurrying overseas to spread the long green across France, England, and Ireland. Horses bought in Kentucky (when the dollar was low) and taken to Europe were now for sale to sensible American shoppers. The peculiar cycle of the racing industry was completed . . . almost. It was the handicapper, with his facts and figures based on strict American measures, who was left out in the cold to fend for himself when it came to European form.

Quinn and others came to the rescue. Foreign races, it turned out, could be judged in much the same manner as American races in terms of class and value. All it took was a code book to translate which were which. Soon, even the most casual handicappers at Belmont and Del Mar knew the difference between a Group I and a Group III race, between a race run at Ayr (in Scotland) and a race run at Longchamp (in Paris). The consideration of all possible information became Quinn's rallying cry.

Graphic Illustrations

A new brand of speed figure tries to capture the subjective subtleties of trip handicapping under a single, numerical umbrella. They originated in a hole-in-the-wall office on New York City's Hudson Street, among a hodgepodge of shops and restaurants bordering Greenwich Village. Meet "The Sheets" of Jerry Brown's Thoro-graph Data Service.

Brown was a disciple of Len Ragosin, who is credited with the genesis of speed figures. People like Brown and Ragosin never go to the racetrack. They analyze results, plot performances, and offer figures subject to broad interpretation. Brown eventually spun off his own company, added a few theoretical twists of his own, and developed a private clientele.

Speed is the overriding obsession. Races are timed privately and from the instant the starting gates open, eliminating the run-up start which is reported as "official" by the track. A race is defined in terms of its speed, and a horse participating in that race is evaluated accordingly. But instead of using the clock as the only criterion, Brown's people factor in several other variables that, they insist, affect the speed of the horse.

Wind. Don't laugh. Just try standing up straight when the wind funnels down the backstretch at Aqueduct from the Atlantic, or howls off the San Francisco Bay onto Golden Gate Fields, or blows the flags stiff at Tampa Bay Downs, hard by the Gulf of Mexico.

Speed figure spotters attempt to be sophisticated in measuring wind. They may use a local weather report (usually from an airport well removed from the racetrack). Or they may simply monitor the flags in the infield, then consult a wind-measure dial. The wind is accounted for and reported in terms relative to other wind measurements at the same track.

Track condition. Simply stated, a 1:10 for 6 furlongs on one day may not be as impressive as a 1:10 for 6 furlongs over the same track on another day. Racing surfaces are the creation of man, and man can alter them dramatically through watering, harrowing, packing, or drying.

"We were absolutely baffled at the variants we were coming up with on the Belmont turf course not long ago," Brown recalled. "We finally found out that the course was being watered in shifts. One part of the course would be watered one evening and the rest of it the next night. So then we had to factor in two different variants for a single race."

Weight. An obvious factor, but one that, according to Brown and others, should have much more bearing over a distance of ground than in sprints.

Lost ground. Spotters isolate on every horse and every race. Given that the shortest distance from Point A to Point B is a straight line (or, on a racetrack, a line skirting the inside rail), the path of each horse is interpreted in terms of "ground lost."

Elapsed time, wind, and track condition help define the characteristics of a given race; weight and lost ground home in on the individual performers. Put them all together and they spell "speed figure." The lower the figure, the better. Perfection, in this world, is zero.

After speed figures are plotted on a calendar graph, the performance history of a horse unfolds. More than a history, however, the graphs reveal an almost biorhythmic picture of highs and lows. Some horses ooze along on a serene plateau, their numbers rarely varying. Others suffer severe spikes in the graph which tend to challenge logical analysis.

"There are people who only look at the last number and bet the horses with the low numbers in each race," Brown said. "The figures are not intended to be used as a straight graph. They should be used as spread figures to predict performance based on recent trends.

"The figures have shown that when a horse runs a race which is far and away the best race of his life, he will tend to 'bounce' off such a stressful effort. Those are the horses you would avoid.

"On the other hand, if a horse has been showing steady improvement—defined by gradually decreasing figures over his last few races—then chances are he will continue to improve in the race at hand. He may be a better bet even though his figure that day is higher than another horse's."

The effect of the stressful effort is a radical approach to numbers handicapping. Cold-hearted numbers can never take into account the physiological impact of a hard race on a fragile thoroughbred. An outstanding effort will follow that horse blindly to the next race, creating the potential for false favorites and unreasonable expectations.

Some horses, however, can handle stressful efforts better than others.

"Our studies show that colts going a route tend not to bounce like sprinting fillies," Brown noted. "But trainers tell us just the opposite. They will say the outstanding route race will take much more out of their horse than the sprint."

Even so, Brown's speed figures have been more popular with horsemen than with ordinary handicappers. Owners and trainers use the "sheets" to claim or buy horses that appear to be on the brink of vast improvement.

"New York bettors don't like to be told what to do," Brown said. "They are very suspicious of new methods, of anything that appears to be cut and dried. So, while the figures are catching on with the private handicappers, we try to cultivate clients among horsemen who use our research to measure progress and soundness."

Brown admits to his share of failures, but on several occasions the figures have led to a jackpot. In early 1985 Brown recommended to a client that he buy a 4-year-old gelding named Tri for Size. The client took his advice, and four months later Tri for Size won the Sword Dancer Handicap, one of New York's most prestigious turf races.

"We actually predicted Tri for Size would win a lot more than he really did," Brown added.

Here are Thoro-graph's figures for the 1986 Belmont Stakes, with the most recent three (main track) numbers for each of the 10 horses in the race:

Bordeaux Bob—15¼, 13½, 11½.
Danzig Connection—15½, 14, 11½.
Ferdinand—10, 7, 5.
Fobby Forbes—11½, 10, 8.
Imperious Spirit—14¾, 10¾, 10½.
Johns Treasure—12½, 9½, 10¾.
Mogambo—8½, 14¼, 8¼.
Parade Marshal—15¼, 13½, 11½.
Personal Flag—13¾, 12, 11.
Rampage—13½, 8½, 8½.

This is clearly not a tout sheet, not when 5 of the 10 have gradually improving numbers and seem to be screaming "Bet me!" in unison. The key is in the interpretation, or so says Brown. After a drastic drop from a 10 to a 7, Ferdinand was expected to "bounce" in his previous race, instead he ran a 5. What now? Rampage and Imperious Spirit had hit plateaus, suggesting they had reached personal peaks. The elevator numbers of Mogambo were typical of his entire season to date. He was hardly reliable.

The horse who apparently ran the most promising race last time out was Danzig Connection, whose 2½-point improvement was impressive without being so dramatic that it could be viewed as too stressful. Fobby Forbes, Parade Marshal, and Personal Flag displayed similar profiles, although their most recent improvements were not as great as that of Danzig Connection. Johns Treasure had apparently reacted to a hard race, the second of the three. The slide in his next race was not drastic, however, so there was reason to believe he would hold fast or improve slightly, rather than slip further.

It was obvious that Ferdinand, rapidly approaching perfection, was the logical choice. Danzig Connection was coming around more rapidly than the others, but even a repeat of his last improvement would not match Ferdinand. Rampage had reached a threatening number and experienced traffic trouble in his last appearance (noted with a "TU" for "took up" on his figure sheet). But he had not raced in five weeks, a definite minus.

So what happened? Danzig Connection won by a length and one-quarter; Johns Treasure finished second, and Ferdinand was a close third. Rampage was the betting favorite and finished seventh, never raising a gallop over a track covered with water from a steady spring rainstorm. Interpretation was the key, but a wet finger in the wind helped.

Oh Boy, an Argument

"The pace of a race hardly ever makes a difference in the outcome," says Jerry Brown. "Maybe once in 30 races. And never in most cases."

Mr. Brown, meet Sam "The Genius" Lewin, who wrote *The Education of a Horseplayer* in 1969 after more than 40 years as one of New York's best-known handicappers.

"There is one maxim I invariably follow in my handicapping," Lewin wrote. "Indeed, it's the keystone of my method. It is: Pace makes the race. By 'pace makes the race' I mean that *the manner in which a race is run determines its outcome* (his italics) . . . .

"Speed that goes unchallenged almost invariably wins. If a horse's past performances show that his times in the early portions of his races are clearly better than those of his competitors, the chances are great that he will open up a commanding lead and his late-running rivals will not be able to catch him. When you see a situation like this, you needn't go further. Unless he clearly lacks stamina, the speed horse is the horse for you to bet.

"Mostly, however, speed does not go unchallenged," Lewin continued. "In most races there are two or even three horses with enough early speed to challenge one another. This often means that the race will be run at a very fast pace, and the speed horses will tire themselves in their early battling. If none of the speed horses in the field has clearly shown that he has the capacity to stand off early challenges and still win, you should bring the come-from-behind horses into your calculations."

Good Ideas

Jeff Siegel agrees with Sam Lewin when it comes to pace. But to properly judge the personality of a given race, a handicapper must become a good race watcher.

"If you have any kind of intelligence and just start watching races, you'll see what works and what doesn't," Siegel says. "There are a few tricks you can use to teach yourself how to watch a race.

"Start by watching a jockey's hands. When a horse is making the lead and the jockey is sitting there with his hands against the reins, the horse is pulling at the bit. The horse probably could go faster if the jock wanted him to.

"Then, when the jockey asks the horse to run, what kind of response does he get? Does the horse pick it up immediately? Or does he just kind of stay at the same pace? When a horse is on the lead, is the jockey pushing and driving, using that horse as hard as he can? If he is, then the horse is probably running as fast as he can. Two horses can both run the first quarter in 22 seconds flat. The numbers say they're the same kind of horse. Visually, you know they may not be. The numbers can't tell you what a horse could have done; they can only tell you what he did.

"A lot of people look for trouble and bet a horse who had big trouble. Well, it all depends on what that trouble is. Was the horse doing anything or going anywhere when he had trouble? Did it prevent him from making a move which would have led to a different outcome of his race? Does a horse overcome adversity to earn his good number? Does a horse win with what looks like a perfect trip? And what's a 'perfect trip'? It could be anything from a horse going to the front with nobody bothering him, to a horse sitting third behind two dueling leaders, or getting through on the inside over a terribly speed-biased inside track.

"Perhaps the most important thing you can learn from watching a race is *how fast a horse can run when he's asked to run*. I look for that horse who can give you that spurt when he is asked."

A Heavy Dose

Pedigree plays an important part in the theories of some handicappers. It is time to look at the most famous theory of them all.

In his column of May 14, 1984, *New York Post* racing writer Ray Kerrison created a monster. He didn't mean to. There was no malevolent intent. He just saw a good angle and went with it. A firestorm of attention followed.

Kerrison was intrigued by a breeding theory known as "Dosage," especially in its application to the Kentucky Derby and Belmont Stakes. At that point, no one in the stands had even heard of the system. It was the exclusive domain of breeders, bloodstock consultants, and professorial bookworms who found their most rapturous moments in the dissection of an intriguing thoroughbred pedigree. Its proponents were Dr. Steve Roman, a physicist with a Houston petrochemical company, and Leon Rasmussen, the suave, silver-haired author of the *Daily Racing Form*'s "Bloodlines" column on racehorse family trees. Kerrison brought them out of the closet with a bang.

"For more than 300 years," he wrote, "horseplayers the world over have been searching for the perfect betting system. It never has been found and it never will be.

"Or so all of us thought. But after this year's Kentucky Derby, that opinion may have to be revised. For the fortieth straight year, the Dosage Index system uncovered the winner. No hustle, no hassle, no gimmick.

"The system is based on pedigree. It has been around for years, and although I've studied it, I still don't understand it entirely. All I know is that it works. But it does more than isolate the potential winner of the Derby. It is unerring in discovering the phony favorite. In that respect it is downright eerie."

Kerrison ticked off a list of the most recent Derby betting favorites that had lost, among them El Baba, Proud Appeal, Air Forbes Won, Muttering, Althea, and Marfa. The Dosage System had, he noted, correctly tabbed as likely Derby winners Sunny's Halo ($7.00 to win),

Swale ($8.80), Pleasant Colony ($9.00) and, in a grand coup, Gato del Sol ($44.40).

Kerrison's column elicited a landslide response. He received "scores of letters" inquiring further about the system. The reason was simple: A foolproof betting system based on pedigree figures to sell like cheap beachfront property. Rasmussen and the *Racing Form* were flooded with requests for copies of the system. "If it works for the Derby, it can work for tomorrow's third race at Bowie!" was the cry.

Kerrison took great pains, in a subsequent column, to defuse the situation. "The Dosage Index is not a betting system as such," he explained. "It was developed principally as a breeding instrument. The betting potential is merely a fringe benefit."

Nevertheless, the bandwagon was rolling. In 1985, Chief's Crown was the pre-Derby favorite despite an indifferent victory over lamentable opposition in the Blue Grass Stakes. As far as the Dosage System was concerned, Chief's Crown could have won the Blue Grass by 31 lengths and set a world record. He had no chance—based on his Dosage numbers—to win the Derby.

Horses with a highly probable chance of winning included Spend A Buck, Stephan's Odyssey, and Proud Truth, and so stated Rasmussen in his popular Derby Day "Bloodlines" column, while throwing Chief's Crown out the window. Spend A Buck won (and paid $10.20), Stephan's Odyssey was second, and Proud Truth was fifth. Chief's Crown swallowed millions of dollars as the 6–5 betting choice and finished third.

(Andrew Rosen, the owner of Chief's Crown, became a believer after the Derby, if he wasn't already. Later that year he asked Rasmussen to analyze the pedigrees of a list of mares waiting to be serviced by Chief's Crown during the colt's first season at stud. Rosen wanted to make sure the offspring were Derby material and measured up to—what else?—the Dosage Index.)

The media pressure on the Dosage System reached hyperboil in 1986. Rasmussen and Roman were deluged with calls and letters throughout the spring from people who wanted to get the inside scoop on their Derby "numbers." From coast to coast, handicappers wanted to know "who couldn't win the Derby" based on the system. Sports editors demanded stories on this latest fad to hit racing, and sports writers had to become instant experts on pedigree and dosage. Even ABC-TV got into the act on the day of the Derby when telecast host

Jim McKay summarized the "very complicated" theory in 22 seconds, complete with splashy graphics.

Syndicated columnist Jim Murray picked up the scent while in Louisville during Derby week. With typical tongue-in-cheek sarcasm he wrote, "It's not a horse's performances that count. It's his ancestors. Does he come from a family that never did a day's work in its life? Never pulled a cart or carried the mail? Is he maybe a bleeder? The equine equivalent of a Hapsburg cadet? A pampered loafer, good only for waltzes and parades?

"You see, racetrack scientists have delved into the pedigrees of winning racehorses and have come up with a common denominator called the Dosage Index, which is kind of the *Almanach De Gotha* for horses, *Burke's Peerage*. If you're not in there, you shouldn't be in the Kentucky Derby, either. Stop cluttering up the ball."

Snow Chief, winner of the Florida Derby and Santa Anita Derby, was the heavy Kentucky Derby favorite. Snow Chief had the wrong Dosage numbers. Rasmussen, in his Derby Day column, picked Ferdinand to win.

Ferdinand won and paid $37.60.

Snow Chief finished eleventh at odds of 9–5.

What the Numbers Mean

"It is not a betting system," Leon Rasmussen insisted once the 1986 Derby dust had settled. "I'm delighted that it continues to work so well when applied to the Kentucky Derby, but I'm always prepared for an exception to the rule."

This was also shortly after Rasmussen cashed a sweet Future Book bet on Ferdinand at odds of 25–1, offered in March when the only thing that stood out about the horse was his pedigree.

That's the thing about the Dosage System—anybody can do it. There is really no trick. The equipment is not that hard to find:

1. A list of the sires considered "leaders of the breed" or "chefs-de-race" by Roman, Rasmussen, and their precursors, Lt. J. J. Vuiller and Dr. Franco Varola. The list, which numbered 164 at the end of 1986, is published each year in the Kentucky Derby edition of the *Daily Racing Form*, and is also available through the mail.

2. A four-generation pedigree of the horse in question. This may take a bit of digging, but pedigrees are regularly published in racing

trade magazines and are among the source materials at the libraries of breeding associations and racetrack publicity departments.

3. The formulas for Dosage Index and its companion figure, Center of Distribution. Neither requires college-level algebra and neither is a secret.

In theory, every horse is influenced by its pedigree. The rigidly controlled breeding of thoroughbreds dictates this to be so. The Dosage theory categorizes a group of stallions, tracing back to the nineteenth century, which influence their offspring in specific ways. Some have sired lines of great speed; others lean toward endurance. Those who transmit the ability to run very fast over a distance of ground (10 to 12 furlongs) are the most desirable of them all.

Once these stallions are identified in a horse's pedigree, the formula goes to work. If there is an abundance of speed-oriented stallion influence coursing through the family of the horse in question, chances are he will have a high Dosage Index number and be an unlikely candidate to handle the 10 furlongs of the Derby or the 12 furlongs of the Belmont Stakes at a fast enough pace. (Through years of study, computer expert Roman established the Dosage Index of 4 as his cutoff point.) Secretariat's Dosage Index was 3.00; Spectacular Bid's flirted with danger at 4.00, while Affirmed (2.08), Seattle Slew (2.14), and Genuine Risk (2.57) were all safely under.

An extremely low number, however, is not necessarily an advantage. "Any horse can get a mile and a quarter if you wait long enough," horsemen like to say. Plodders who amble along at one moderate pace are of value only as allowance horses or claimers. The ideal Dosage Index number is 1. In the last 20 years, the Kentucky Derby winner with the Dosage Index closest to the ideal was Canonero II, at 1.29. Canonero, who came from Venezuela, is also generally regarded as the greatest handicapping surprise in the modern history of the race.

The Center of Distribution further defines the horse. The Dosage Index can be below 4 but sometimes the pedigree is badly tipped toward sires of great speed, a no-no. A Center of Distribution number of zero is ideal, but anything up to 1.25 is acceptable when hunting for a Derby or Belmont winner.

More often the opposite will occur. Consider the 1986 Derby: Ferdinand's Dosage Index was 1.50 and his Center of Distribution was .55. The favorite, Snow Chief, had an acceptable Center of Distribution of .67, but his Dosage Index strayed over the line to 5.00. (Because of this as well as Snow Chief's outstanding credentials, Rasmussen was a bit nervous. "An anomaly on pedigree," he called Snow Chief. "Could be the first of his kind [in terms of dosage] to win the Derby.")

Had Rasmussen and Roman been promoting their theories in 1967 they would have come out against the chances of the heavily favored Damascus in the Kentucky Derby, an idea tantamount to taking the Lakers against the Celtics at Boston Garden . . . and giving points.

Damascus lost the Derby, finishing third to Proud Clarion (DI 1.60, CD .40, win price $62.20), but he won just about every other race that season and was named Horse of the Year. Among his victories was the Belmont Stakes, which saddled the dosage system with one of only two "high DI" exceptions since 1940 (the other was Conquistador Cielo in 1982). Trainer Frank Whiteley always maintained that Damascus lost the Derby because he was not accompanied in the post parade by his stable pal Pumpkin, a little palomino who was kind of a four-legged security blanket for the great champion. With 100,000 screaming fans and no Pumpkin, Damascus was a nervous wreck and ran like a horse who wanted to hide. Was that the real reason? Deep, down inside, Damascus may have been dialing the wrong number, and it had nothing to do with his Dosage.

Will Dosage Say When Not to Play?

In spite of the protests by its originators, the Dosage System can, on occasion, wave a red flag of warning when considering a particular horse. And since there are so few races to which Dosage analysis pertains, its methods could be considered a handicapping tool . . . if you want to put in the work.

Dosage applies only to races of one and one-quarter miles or more, with horses carrying equal weights or weights that are assigned on the basis of age. Several of North America's top races fall into this category, including the Travers, Jockey Club Gold Cup, Beldame Stakes, three of the seven Breeders' Cup races, and most of the major autumn turf races. However, on a day-in, day-out basis at most racetracks, such events are rare. Races at a mile and one-quarter and beyond tend to be less competitive, with the fields diluted by horses who cannot cope with the distance.

To illustrate the possible handicapping application of the Dosage System, let's look at two races run in 1985. The first is a maiden event for 3-year-old fillies at 1¼ miles on the Belmont turf course. Each of the 10 entrants carried 118 pounds. The other race is a $20,000 claimer at Saratoga, run at a mile and one-quarter on the main track. The weights stretch the qualifications a bit (the eight runners were assigned between 112 and 117 pounds), but even Rasmussen would allow us to proceed in the name of research.

First, a step-by-step stroll through a Dosage analysis. Finding out the Dosage Index and the Center of Distribution will tell us whether or not the horse passes or fails the distance test.

Consider the filly in post position No. 1 in the Belmont Park filly race. Her name is Winter's Realm. Her sire is Key to the Kingdom, and her dam is Winter Memory, a daughter of Olden Times. Her four-generation male family looks like this:

1st Generation	2nd Generation	3rd Generation	4th Generation
Key to the Kingdom	BOLD RULER Olden Times	NASRULLAH PRINCEQUILLO Relic Nearctic	NEARCO DISCOVERY PRINCE ROSE WAR ADMIRAL War Relic DJEBEL NEARCO NATIVE DANCER

Each of the stallions in capital letters is a chef-de-race, the only ones we pay attention to when dealing in dosage. Each of the "chefs" fits one of the five descriptive categories of stallions (Brilliant, Intermediate, Classic, Solid, Professional), or a combination of two categories. For instance, Bold Ruler is considered a "Brilliant–Intermediate" sire, while Prince Rose is simply "Classic."

The closer a stallion is to the first generation, the more influence he will have on the Dosage calculations (in a 2, 4, 8, 16 progression). Points are assigned to each of the five categories based on the appearance of a stallion that fits the label. In the case of a "combination" stallion, the points are split between the two categories. Here, then, is how the major influential stallions in the family tree of Winter's Realm are arranged, with points included:

Brilliant		Intermediate		Classic	
Bold Ruler	4	Bold Ruler	4	Nearco	1
Nasrullah	4	Princequillo	2	Prince Rose	2
Nearco	1	Djebel	2	War Admiral	2
Nearco	1	Native Dancer	1	Nearco	1
Total	10	Total	9	Native Dancer	1
				Total	7

Solid	Professional
Princequillo 2	none
Discovery 2	Total 0
Total 4	

The Dosage "Profile" is made up of the five totals: 10-9-7-4-0. To find the Dosage Index, divide the left half of the profile by the right half (splitting the 7 in two): 22.5 / 7.5 = 3.00. The Center of Distribution figure is a bit more complex. Double the Brilliant and Professional totals; add the Brilliant to the Intermediate, then subtract the Solid and the Professional. Divide the resulting total by the sum of the five numbers in the original Dosage Profile. In the case of Winter's Realm, the calculation looks like this:

$$\frac{([10 \times 2] + 9) - (4 + [0 \times 2])}{(10 + 9 + 7 + 4 + 0)} = 0.83$$

The following is the field of fillies from our sample race, with Dosage Index and Center of Distribution figures alongside. Remember, the people who thought this up tell us we should throw out any horses with DI's over 4.00 and CD's over 1.25 if we want a horse to run a competitive mile and one-quarter.

Horse	DI	CD
Winter's Realm	3.00	0.83
Our Lady Jeanne	2.25	0.62
Bourbon and Honey	1.12	0.11
Royal Extravagance	1.05	0.00
Lead Runner	2.69	0.71
Shiitake	1.43	0.26
Isn't She Nice	1.67	0.50
Glorious Calling	1.44	0.34
Honorary Doctorate	1.15	0.21
Manderley	4.18	0.80

In this case, the Dosage System was not much help with throwouts. All but Manderley qualify on both DI and CD, and Manderley fails on DI only. One thing that does jump up, however, is the near perfection of Royal Extravagance. In the world of Dosage, a DI of 1.00 is the ideal, and a CD of 0.00 makes grown men swoon. Only two of the 10 fillies in this field had run as far as 1¼ miles before, and Royal Extravagance was not one of them. There she is, her Dosage numbers near perfection and getting her first shot at the distance she deserves. A believer in the theories of Dosage analysis could never let this one slip by.

Royal Extravagance finished sixth at odds of 34–1. Isn't She Nice won and paid $7.80 for a $2 win bet. Manderley finished fifth, nearly 4 lengths in front of Royal Extravagance.

One race does not a theory prove, nor disprove. But at least we have walked through the Dosage System together. How about one more for the road? The field of eight in the one and one-quarter mile claimer at Saratoga revealed the following DIs and CDs:

Horse	DI	CD
Columbia Pride	5.18	1.15
Excommunicate	1.22	0.47
Take a Mile	2.67	0.86
Run Shanley	1.20	0.22
What Nonsense	4.71	0.98
Deedee's Deal	3.31	0.93
Heavenly Writer	2.69	0.71
Feeling Too Much	3.00	2.00

The numbers label Feeling Too Much, Columbia Pride, and What Nonsense as questionable to get the distance. Nobody is perfect, but Run Shanley comes the closest. So what happened? Heavenly Writer caught Deedee's Deal and Run Shanley in the stretch to win by a half-length and pay $13.60. What Nonsense finished fourth, beaten 10½ lengths, Feeling Too Much finished fifth, and Columbia Pride ran dead last.

In both examples, the horses that couldn't win—based on Dosage—didn't win. It still seems like a lot of work to narrow the field by one or two horses; but if one of the horses thrown out on Dosage is a betting favorite, the opportunity for profit increases. It is still up to the individual bettor to come up with the right answer from other sources. Maybe we should listen to Rasmussen after all. Handicapping with the Dosage System may be like studying Einstein before changing a tire.

What You See is What You Get

If that last little exercise left you scratching your head, now it's time to unwind with the lighter side of handicapping. Screenwriter, biographer, and part-time handicapper Maurice Zolotow contributed an invaluable volume to the literature of thoroughbred racing entitled *Confessions of a Racetrack Fiend*. The names of celebrities are liberally dropped between the covers (the book is dedicated to Martin Ritt and Walter Matthau), and the tone is that of a not-so-innocent abroad in the strange world of racing.

Zolotow was particularly intrigued by the ideas of Beatrice Lydecker, who at that time was gaining some recognition for her "equine sensory perception" theories. Zolotow put Lydecker's emphasis on thoroughbred body language to work and came up with a few R-rated observations of his own:

"1. Tail up. A horse whose tail is up is feeling tense. The conventional wisdom holds that this tension counts heavily against him in a sprint race. In a longer race, a mile or more, if the horse is a class animal, he will work out his nervousness and you shouldn't be deterred from betting him if you like him. Personally, I do not set much store by "tail up." If the animal isn't leaping around and acting restless, so fractious that the grooms can't hold him, I won't let a tail-up manifestation deter me from betting him, if I like him in other respects.

"2. Washiness. This refers to copious perspiration all over the horse. Again, this is a sign of nervousness. While I would rather not see my horse washy, as long as he is acting calm, I will bet him. Often competitors, animals or human, go out feeling tension, even fear, and give great performances. One of the greatest actors in the history of the American theatre, Alfred Lunt, once told me that toward the end of his stage career . . . he was so nervous before he made his first entrance that he always vomited in the wings! You'd never know it when you saw his ease and power on the stage.

"3. Bandages. Sometimes horses have bandages on their front legs and sometimes on their rear legs. Again, I'm not crazy about betting a horse who might have a serious condition requiring bandages, but I believe that in most cases, from what they tell me, these wrappers are put on for skin protection or minor support. Owners and trainers would not risk an expensive animal in a race if he were not in reasonably fit condition. . . . There's also the possibility that an owner has ordered his trainer to put bandages on a claiming horse—to deter a claim!

"4. Erection. What about a colt who has a hard-on? This is a very bad sign. As a veteran track acquaintance of mine says, 'Such a horse has his mind on f---ing, not winning, and if I bet on him, I'll be the one that gets f---ed.'

"5. Voiding the bowels. Once in a while you see a horse on his way to the gate pausing to take a crap. Or he might move his bowels in the paddock. Aside from displaying bad manners, this horse may be telling us that he has been given a bag of oats recently, which is not a good sign. He may also be so relaxed that he is not terribly eager to run a race. He may just be in the mood to go back to his stall and stretch out and nuzzle his stable companion, a goat or dog or small pony.

"On the other hand, you might notice that the horse who has voided has a look of eager power about him, as if he feels so good about it that he now wants to show the world how he can run. In this case the horse would be a sure thing, especially if he had a good track record."

Terror for Profit

Thoroughbreds are naturally fearful animals, and yet that fear can sometimes be turned into our advantage. I've always been convinced that some horses are competing out of sheer terror—fear of failure, injury, or even death. Call it primal handicapping.

In early 1985, parapsychologist Nancy Regalmuto was hired by *Equus* magazine to "communicate" with John Henry. The 10-year-old gelding had just been acclaimed Horse of the Year for the second time; he was out of training with a ligament injury, and he had suddenly (after five glorious seasons) become a mass media freak. *People* magazine had named him one of the 20 most fascinating personalities of 1984.

Regalmuto gave John Henry the once over, made a few observations concerning "energy blockages" and "raw physical strength." Then, in her transcription of the hour-long "conversation" with John Henry, she revealed some shocking insights. Among them:

• John Henry was convinced he would never retire and that he would break down at some point.

• He was traumatized at a young age by the euthanasia of an injured stablemate who had not won enough to be worth saving.

• After that, he came to believe he was "living on borrowed time" (according to John Henry) and that his only chance for survival was to win.

John Henry was too professional to let his fear show through, if indeed he was afraid of failure. But I did witness first hand the positive effects of terror upon a racehorse.

The best thoroughbred John Gosden ever trained—perhaps ever will train—was a filly named Royal Heroine. In March of 1984, she and two other horses fell in a race at Santa Anita. Only Royal Heroine survived. After nine weeks of recuperation, she came back to the races with vengeance. Her most glorious moment came in the Breeders' Cup Mile, less than eight months after her accident, when she easily defeated the best field the world could offer. Her time that day was 1:32⅖, the fastest mile ever run by a female racehorse.

Gosden had to be half mentor, half psychiatrist with Royal Heroine. According to the trainer, she was never quite the same emotionally after the incident at Santa Anita.

"You could see it in her eyes, especially while she was running," Gosden recalls. "It was a look of fear, of sheer terror, as if she remembered every detail of that terrible day. And the only way to get that horrible vision behind her was to get the ordeal over with as quickly as possible. So she ran as fast as she could, but I saw no joy in her running."

Ever since then, I have bet on scared horses. Energized by their fear, adrenalized to the gills, they run from the deepest wells of courage.

Happy Birthday, Baby

Believe it or not, there are people who chart the astrological personalities of thoroughbred racehorses. Virginia Reames, astrologist and accomplished horsewoman, observed in *Equus* magazine that the most important event in John Henry's early history was when he was gelded. "Astrologically speaking, the castration sent John Henry's energy flow to his feet," was her analysis.

On the face of it, this sounds like a harmless exercise, to be regarded with the same level of concern given astrology readings over morning coffee. "If it sounds good, believe it" is how most of us regard our daily signs. But in the case of thoroughbreds it is pitiful folly.

Why? Because there is nothing random about thoroughbred intercourse, and therefore the "stars" at the end of the gestation period are severely limited. There are no Leos, Virgos, Libras, Scorpios, or Sagittarians, and precious few Capricorns and Moon Children among the thoroughbred population. The births of racehorses are arranged so that deliveries take place in the first six months of the year, and ideally in February, March, and April. "We don't do any breeding past June 20," said the manager of a prominent California farm. "Don't want to keep the foaling staff around any longer than we have to." So much for the mysterious relationship between horse and heavens.

Within the limited calendar of thoroughbred conception, however, there is something to be said for when a horse is born. There was a fascinating episode of the British mystery series "The Racing Game" in which a thoroughbred was delivered a few minutes before midnight on December 31. His desperate owner subsequently lied about the birth, recording a January 1 foaling date. The horse became a world beater as a 3-year-old and was on his way to becoming a champion when the scandal was uncovered.

Why all the fuss over a few minutes late one wintry night? Racehorses, no matter when they are actually born, are assigned the universal birthdate of January 1. If a horse is born in May, he will celebrate his first birthday seven months later. The motive for the falsified birthdate in the television drama becomes clear. The young horse born on December 31 would be considered a yearling the very next day. A year and a day later he would be lumped with the 2-year-olds of his generation, even though his body clock had ticked off less than 13 months. He would always be physically behind his classmates.

But, if he were a January 1 baby, he would have the full year to grow before becoming a yearling. By the time he went to the races as a 2-year-old or 3-year-old, he would be several months ahead of his contemporaries in physical development, since most of them would have been born in March, April, or May.

Since most responsible owners plan their matings to end the gestation period safely after the first of the year, the plot of the mystery was a bit preposterous. Yet it did underline the perception that "early" foals have a tremendous advantage over "late" foals.

Do Early Birds Get All the Worms?

Handicappers can find an edge by knowing the actual birthdates of thoroughbreds, but the knowledge can only be applied in a small percentage of races—early 2-year-old races. After that, the effects of early or late foal dates seem to evaporate.

It is simple enough for the average racing fan and handicapper to find out the actual birthdate of a horse. The Jockey Club in Lake Success, New York, has a customer service telephone line expressly devoted to such research. Give them the name of the horse (or its dam) along with the year it was foaled and within seconds they'll have the foal date.

Now what? Well, it stands to reason that older horses will not be significantly affected by their actual age when competing against contemporaries. In human terms, a 25-year-old athlete would seem to have no particular advantage over a 22-year-old athlete. But at a younger level there can be dramatic differences. The idea of a 19-year-old going one-on-one with a 16-year-old in anything (other than gymnastics or tiddlywinks) is downright unfair.

The lifespan of a thoroughbred is only about one-third that of a human, and his competitive life as a professional athlete is even more compressed. Any edge in maturity—months, even weeks—could be an advantage for a racehorse. To illustrate this theory, let us review the lists of outstanding 2-year-olds and 3-year-olds of 1985 studied in a previous chapter. Take special note of the birthdate in relation to the final rating:

2-YEAR-OLD COLTS

Name	Date of Birth	Rating
Hilco Scamper	Feb. 10	7th
Pillaster	Feb. 16	8th
Darby Fair	Feb. 25	18th
Southern Appeal	Feb. 26	20th
Storm Cat	Feb. 27	3rd
Papal Power	Feb. 27	10th
Admiral's Image	Feb. 27	17th
Electric Blue	March 1	6th
Groovy	March 9	14th
Meadowlake	March 12	1st
Ferdinand	March 12	19th
Ketoh	March 14	9th
Ogygian	March 17	4th
Snow Chief	March 17	5th
Mogambo	March 17	13th
Sovereign Don	March 20	16th
Danzig Connection	April 6	15th
Tasso	April 20	2nd
Swear	May 8	11th
Scat Dancer	May 11	12th

2-YEAR-OLD FILLIES

Name	Date of Birth	Rating
Silent Account	Jan. 22	10th
Nervous Baba	Feb. 11	15th
Parquill	Feb. 17	13th
Funistrada	Feb. 24	9th
Pamela Key	Feb. 24	17th
Family Style	Feb. 27	2nd
Musical Lark	March 1	7th
Guadery	March 17	8th
Twilight Ridge	March 20	1st
Steal a Kiss	March 20	12th
I'm Sweets	March 26	4th
Really Fancy	March 28	16th
Deep Silver	March 28	18th
Arewehavingfunyet	March 29	5th
Cadabra Abra	April 9	20th
Laz's Joy	April 18	19th
Cosmic Tiger	May 1	14th
I'm Splendid	May 11	3rd
Trim Colony	May 11	11th
Lazer Show	May 31	6th

The cliché is that female thoroughbreds develop faster than males. It just so happens that this small sampling supports the theory, indicating that late 2-year-old filly foals overcome their birthdates better than late colts racing at that age. Two of the very best 2-year-old fillies of 1985 were I'm Splendid (born May 11) and Lazer Show (May 31). Neither seemed to be at a disadvantage because of their foal dates. At the same time, there were two May foals among the 20 juvenile colts in the study group—Swear (May 8) and Scat Dancer (May 11)—but neither one made the top 10 in ratings.

Since no serious breeder likes to cut it much closer than February, it was not surprising to find only one January foal. However, the 2-year-old racehorse is very much a work in progress. Dramatic physical changes evolve over weeks, not months. If an owner has a horse showing ability early in its 2-year-old season, you can bet he or she will be delighted if it also has a February or early March foal date. Every little bit of physical maturity helps. One thing is certain: When it comes to picking winners in the early round of 2-year-old races, the betting fan would be wise to have actual foal dates as part of his repetoire. The older the foal, the better.

(There is just such a movement, which started two years ago in

California with "Pedigree Lines" in the daily track program on races for maiden 2-year-olds. The brainchild of Jay Woodward, former chart caller for the *Daily Racing Form*, these lines include foal date, stud fee of the sire, and an abbreviated description of the dam as a racehorse and as a producer of racehorses.)

Do the same trends exist among 3-year-olds? Are fillies the early bloomers? Do early foals have an advantage? Here are the foal dates for the top 20-rated 3-year-olds in the colt and filly study groups, including those listed as turf or sprint specialists:

3-YEAR-OLD COLTS

Name	Date of Birth	Rating
Danger's Hour	Feb. 13	14th
Skywalker	March 4	7th
Banner Bob	March 4	16th
Proud Truth	March 11	2nd
Another Reef	March 12	18th
Stephan's Odyssey	March 16	10th
Shadeed	March 21	4th
Rhoman Rule	March 21	9th
Eternal Prince	March 21	17th
Smile	March 26	12th
Chief's Crown	April 7	3rd
Creme Fraiche	April 7	6th
Turkoman	April 11	19th
Imperial Choice	April 17	13th
Noble Fighter	April 22	15th
Pancho Villa	April 27	11th
Tank's Prospect	May 2	5th
Spend A Buck	May 15	1st
Baillamont	May 19	20th
Skip Trial	May 31	8th

3-YEAR-OLD FILLIES

Name	Date of Birth	Rating
Magnificent Lindy	Feb. 20	10th
Dawn's Curtsey	Feb. 25	20th
Fran's Valentine	Feb. 26	2nd
Videogenic	March 8	16th
Bessarabian	March 9	9th
Mom's Command	March 14	1st
Kamikaze Rick	March 17	4th
Koluctoo's Jill	March 18	7th
Wising Up	March 22	17th

Name	Date of Birth	Rating
Rascal Lass	April 6	11th
Lady's Secret	April 8	3rd
Clock's Secret	April 8	13th
Marshua's Echelon	April 18	8th
Savannah Slew	April 21	6th
Lucy Manette	May 3	14th
Le L'Argent	May 13	12th
Tabayour	May 13	15th
Jolly Saint	May 13	19th
Lady on the Run	May 14	18th
Devalois	May 29	5th

By the age of 3, the colts apparently have caught up with the fillies. Three of the best of that generation—Spend A Buck, Tank's Prospect, and Skip Trial—were May foals, while five of the six May foals among 3-year-old fillies were well down the list.

Based on the foal-date tendencies of these leading 2- and 3-year-olds of 1985, one of two assumptions can be made by handicappers, owners, breeders, and trainers. Take your pick:

1. Once in possession of an early foal (February or March), an owner or trainer will tend to treat the horse as a potential early winner. Handicappers equipped with foal dates would be wise to go along with the perception. Whether or not the young horse stands the early pressure and is able to fulfill expectations is up to its class and physical maturity. No matter what the outcome, however, it was destined to be tested early because of its birthdate.

2. The dramatically higher number of April and May birthdates among the top 3-year-olds suggests that earlier foals were burned out as 2-year-olds, before they entered their second season of competition. April and May foals, held back at 2, ended up at the top of their 3-year-old class. Only one February foal (the California-bred filly Fran's Valentine) made the top 10 as a 3-year-old.

There are always the exceptions. A top horse disregards such accidental occurrences as birthdate and circumstance. Spend A Buck, the 3-year-old champion and Horse of the Year who sold for a song as part of a bankruptcy dispersal, was an outstanding 2-year-old despite his May 15 foal date.

Blow Out the Candles

It's no secret how Derby Wish got his name. He was foaled on May 1, 1982, the day of the Kentucky Derby. On Derby Day three years later, Derby Wish was at Churchill Downs . . . but not for the Kentucky Derby. Seems he forgot to live up to his name.

For the hardcore numerologists in the crowd there were some unavoidable hunch bets in 1985. Most of them were a bust. Just Anything went postward in the Ruffian Handicap at Sportsman's Park on her third birthday, April 6, and finished third (that figures) at odds of 3–5. Don't Say Halo, another April 6 foal, ran the worst race of his budding young career on that date in the Santa Anita Derby. Lucy Manette, 19–1 longshot against some of the best fillies in the country, celebrated her third birthday on May 3 by finishing fourth in the Kentucky Oaks. Gate Dancer, who must have been born under a bad sign, finished last in a six-horse San Luis Rey Stakes field on his fourth birthday, March 31, at 2–1.

There were some happy endings. The old battler Western ran so hard to finish second in the prestigious San Luis Rey Stakes on March 31 that he hurt himself and spent the night of his seventh birthday in pain. The French turf horse Bob Back left town on his fourth birthday, May 26, and celebrated in style by winning the Premio Presidente della Repubblica in Rome. Forzando, born in England on February 11, 1981, ended up at Santa Anita Park in the Sierra Madre Handicap exactly four years later. It was party time for his backers, who collected at nearly 12–1 odds when the birthday boy won the race.

And amazingly enough, Videogenic, who ran 26 times during 1985, did *not* compete on her birthday, March 8.

The Real Payoff

Handicapping gives the racing fan a chance to crawl under the skin of racing and emerge with a vested interest. It doesn't matter if you bet on birthdays, speed figures, newspaper tips, or the horse with the longest tail. The thrill is in the hunt, and the payoff cannot be matched in any other sport. As Jeff Siegel describes:

"There are two things that make racing enjoyable. One is winning money. The other is winning money with your own picks. There is nothing more gratifying or ego-serving than to handicap a card, bet your own picks, and win your own money. That's fun. That's wonderful! You're not trying to make a living. You're not trying to change your life. You are out there to have a good time, read the *Form*, win some money, and drive home that night thinking you're the smartest sonofagun that ever lived. That's why people should try to teach themselves to handicap the horses."

3

Can't Live With 'Em, Can't Live Without 'Em: The Jockeys

We have amongst us a school of skinny dwarfs whose leaders are paid better than the greatest statesmen in Europe. The commonest jockey boy in this company of mannikins can usually earn more than the average scholar or professional man, and the whole set receive a good deal more of adulation than has been bestowed on any soldier, sailor, explorer or scientific man of our generation.
> —*James Runciman,* Contemporary Review, *1889*

Never trust a guy who wears a size three hat.
> —Charlie Whittingham

A famous trainer once pointed to a group of 20 celebrated jockeys gathered around a podium for an awards presentation.

"You've got more thieves standing there than Robin Hood had in Sherwood Forest," he said.

He was kidding . . . sort of. Trainers harbor a natural animosity toward jockeys which stems from the taproots of ego, fame, and fortune. Jockeys spend 20 minutes with a horse and get all the glory, then forget about the animal as soon as they dismount. Trainers are up before dawn seven days a week playing nursemaid to fragile legs and evil temperaments. In the garden paddocks of Santa Anita Park in Arcadia, California, there are commemorative statues of three famous jockeys: Bill Shoemaker, John Longden, and George Woolf. There are no statues of trainers.

Then again, no trainer was ever trampled to death in front of 40,000 people. Since the Jockeys' Guild was chartered in 1941, there have been 121 recorded riding fatalities. Life insurance rates for jockeys rank right up there with Formula I racecar drivers, bullfighters, and skydivers.

Racing fans also find themselves at constant odds with jockeys . . . especially losing fans. In no other sport does money move so freely through a crowd. Racing fans have a vested interest in every nuance of the action. Baseball fanatics may bet on every pitch, but the practice has yet to be institutionalized. And in no other sport (save perhaps professional golf) are the athletes so accessible to angry fans. When was the last time someone threw a beer at Tom Watson for missing a three-foot putt?

During the first six years of the 1980s, North American trainers sent out an average of 72,557 different thoroughbreds each year to run in an average of 71,955 different races across the country. Every one of those horses had a rider—at least when it entered the starting gate. Racing fans bellied up to the windows to bet $46,523,594,940 over the same period. You've got to trust somebody sometime.

Which jockeys have proven the most trustworthy? Walk through a racetrack crowd and the answer will usually be "the guy that won the last race for me." An hour later the same jockey will have fallen from grace. A disgruntled fan at Pimlico for the 1986 Preakness Stakes tore up his tickets on Badger Land and called his rider, Hall of Famer Jorge Velasquez, "the most overrated of the top jockeys." Never mind that Badger Land was the most overrated of the 3-year-olds at the time. When Laffit Pincay returned to the saddle one month after the suicide of his wife in January of 1985, the fans at Santa Anita had tears in their eyes, cheering him on. One year later, as Pincay wallowed in the throes of a losing slump, the same people spit on his boots, called him names, and threw torn tickets at him as he passed. I will always have a soft spot in my heart for an apprentice named Benny DiNicola, who finished second on a filly at 33–1 in an exacta race at Del Mar. I cashed the exacta, and renamed my cat Nicole. Believe me, I couldn't tell you who rode the winner.

Our purpose here is not to isolate the best jockeys of a particular year and carve their names in granite. You'll see just how difficult it is to name "the best" among jockeys, no matter what method of comparison you use. Most importantly, the statistical analyses that follow can be adapted to any racing venue. We will look at the strengths and weaknesses of a group of jockeys considered best, but you can look for the same tendencies in the jockeys at your local track.

Our sources for statistics on jockeys are abundant. The *Daily Rac-*

ing Form publishes everything you need to know when it comes to the nuts and bolts of who won what and where. On a local basis, every respectable racetrack prints current jockey standings in the daily program (at least for the top 10 local riders). There are also publications cropping up in major racing centers that keep track of the winning percentages of all jockeys.

Beyond these sources, the individual handicapper can keep track of his own special interests. Handicapping specialists sometimes home in on certain types of races, and following the records of the jockeys riding in those races is part of their discipline. A computer with a simple calculation program is a handy tool, but there's nothing wrong with using good old longhand notes on graph paper to keep track of the jockeys in turf races, maiden races, or whatever category you choose.

The Categories

Who says America is a classless society? The caste system is alive and thriving in thoroughbred racing. Racetrack programs are designed to pit horses of reasonably equal abilities. Only special exceptions stray successfully upward. Just ask anyone who tries to make a living betting maidens against winners, claimers against stakes horses, or even fillies against colts.

Owners, trainers, and the public can circumvent the class system. They have the luxury to pick and choose the type of horse on which they spend their time and money. The vast majority of jockeys, on the other hand, must ride them all. (Jockeys are not under contract. They live a "no play, no pay" way of life.) On a given day a jockey may be faced with nine different kinds of horse, each one requiring a different touch. The general categories are these:

Maidens. A charming term, blatantly sexual and courtesy of Old England, referring to horses (both male and female) who have yet to experience the ectasy of winning. Maiden races make up 20 percent to 25 percent of American racing programs, depending on the time of year.

Claimers. These horses are for sale, to be "claimed" after a race for a price set before the race. Talk about caveat emptor! If a claimer wins, the former owner takes home the prize. If a claimer breaks down, the new owner foots the bill for repair or, in some sad cases, humane destruction. Claimers come from all walks of equine life. Prices range from less than $1,000 to a gimmicky $1,000,000 in special New York and Los Angeles claiming events. Some claimers once were stars, now unsound beyond recognition. Others never caught the spark at all. They are the cannon fodder of the game, grist for the pari-mutuel machine. Their races make up 40 percent to 50 percent of most programs.

Quality. The greatest range of runners, beginning with those who have just won their first race to the game's foremost performers. The best way to judge the quality of a race is by the size of its purse.

Depending upon the whims of the racing secretary, quality races may show any number of personalities. They might be called allowances, overnight handicaps, restricted stakes, graded stakes, invitationals, starter handicaps, or futurities.

In terms of purse value and prestige, quality races run the gamut from $4,000 "nonwinners other than maiden" to the multimillion-dollar Breeders' Cup events. To fairly reflect riding tendencies in quality races, three divisions will be considered: Class C ($39,999 purse or less), Class B ($40,000–$99,999 purse) and Class A ($100,000 and upward).

Class C races run the gamut of "conditioned allowances." In English, that means anything that's not a claimer or a stakes race. These are designed to bring together horses of relatively equal abilities, narrowly defining eligibility in such specific parlance as "for fillies and mares, 3-year-olds and upward that have not won $5,000 twice since July 3, 1985, in maiden, claiming, or starter handicap races."

Class C races will also include most stakes races at minor tracks and a very minor stakes races at major tracks. In 1985, 29 percent of all North American stakes races offered between $25,000 and $49,999.

Class B races comprise the majority of the stakes races offered at the top racetracks in New York, California, Florida, New Jersey, Maryland, and the Midwest. The average stakes purse in 1985 was $51,631, according to *The Blood-Horse* magazine.

Class A races, $100,000 and up, are always stakes. In 1985, 12 percent of all stakes races had a value of $100,000 or more. The winner gets in the neighborhood of $60,000 for winning a hundred-grander, which translates into $6,000 for the jockey. Not bad for 10 minutes of work.

Under the umbrellas of maiden, claiming, and quality races fall certain subcategories: sprints and routes, grass and dirt, male and female. The sex split in races leans approximately 55 percent to 45 percent in favor of males. There are more males in the racing population because the breeding business requires only one stallion per approximately 30 mares, and males who have no future at stud can be castrated to keep them in the racing population. The frequency of sprint, route, turf, and dirt racing depends greatly upon the physical setup of the racecourses themselves and to a lesser extent upon the nature of the local horse population.

Modern thoroughbreds are asked to run anywhere from 2 furlongs (a quarter of a mile) to 2½ miles. It takes specialized animals to excel at each distance, and they are bred, raised, and trained with just such specific performances in mind.

At one end of the spectrum there are the instant accelerators, horses who blast from the gate and run as fast as they can for as far as they can. At the other end are the route horses, possessing stamina and the ability to ration speed over a distance of ground. The dividing line between sprints and routes is commonly drawn at 7 furlongs, but there are exceptions. The 6½-furlong turf race at Santa Anita Park often plays very much like a route race. Distance horses are not as compromised by sharp turns as they are in main-track sprints. On the other hand, the one-turn mile race at Hollywood Park is becoming known as the longest sprint in North America. California racing is (in)famous for its style of fly early and fade late. Instead of copying the slow-starting, one-turn mile techniques of jockeys in Chicago and New York, California riders treat the HollyMile like a 7-furlong race with a furlong gut check at the end.

Given this variety of race and racehorse classifications, it may be unreasonable to expect every jockey to master each type of animal and every situation. Our study of riding statistics for 1985 will deliver portraits of top jockeys in terms of their winning percentage in sprints (short races), routes (long races), maiden races, claimers, quality events, turf races, and filly races.

On the local level, there are many other possible categories of measurement, or subcategories of those suggested here. That is the beauty of handicapping. The handicapper makes his own rules. And when comparing the strengths and weaknesses of jockeys, there are any number of dimensions that could be analyzed.

The kind of races a jockey wins depends upon several factors. Of course, there is his overall ability and the perception of that ability by the owners and trainers who are his employers. Beyond that, success or failure depends upon factors that are difficult to measure, but important for the handicapper to take into account. Among them are:

1. Stable connections. With so many trainers in the business, many riders prefer to establish close ties with a handful of stables and take

advantage of a steady relationship for steady work. The downside is obvious. When a stable begins doing badly because of illness, injuries, or just plain bad karma, the statistics of the stable jockey will suffer as well. A jockey may not be riding as badly as his statistics indicate because of such associations.

2. The jockey agent. Just as there are good and bad jockeys, there are good and bad jockey agents. These are the people who arrange the mounts, working from a "condition book" of races that resembles a cross between a menu in a Chinese restaurant and *The New York Times* crossword. The best agents cut through the tangle of the condition book. They know just which horses will fit which races and whether or not they will be ready to run. The bad agents are lost in the shuffle, picking up the scraps.

Jockeys change agents like George Steinbrenner changes managers, but sometimes they do it after considerable damage to their business and reputation has already occurred. If a jockey's stats begin to slip, take a look at the kinds of horses he has been riding. Are the odds consistently high? Are they rarely in contention? And then watch the columns of the local press for the announcement of an agent switch.

3. Personality. An aggressive, excitable jockey may be well suited to the short-term pressure of sprint races, but he may not be able to handle the subtle demands of longer races, when patience and prudence can make the difference between winning or losing. Get to know your local jockeys by watching them closely as they come out for a race and return after a race. Racing is no different from other high-speed sports. It can be a very emotional game for the participants. The jockeys who handle their emotions best usually win the most often.

Measuring Sticks

Where is my man Benny DiNicola today? Riding in the backwater of America's racetracks, probably making a decent living, far, far away from the hot lights of Broadway. The "best" jockeys should not be measured with the heart, or with unreliable memory. The best must stand tall when judged in the light of several important categories, year in, year out. Those benchmarks include:

Money. Racing's basic equation is very simple. The tracks that generate the greatest amount of betting can offer the highest purses and therefore lure the best, most consistent horses, which in turn attract the greatest amount of betting. Drawn inexorably to this cyclical flame are the best riders—or at least the riders who think they are the best and want to cash in.

Winners. There are big fish in small ponds all over the racing world. The truly talented do not necessarily end up in the megacenters of New York and southern California, where 25 percent of North America's $652,475,303 in prize money was disbursed in 1985. The leading riders in Maryland, Chicago, southern Florida, San Francisco, and Kentucky will rarely penetrate the top money lists; but they will, because of their dominance of the local market, finish high each year in number of sheer winners.

Specialists. Peel back the skin of any list of jockeys—local or national—and the revelations come dripping out. One jockey is a superior rider of turf races. Another peaks in big money events. Yet another is a solid race-by-race journeyman. Gamblers, owners, and trainers observe such tendencies—either by instinct or documentation—to weed through jockeys and make important fiscal decisions.

Awards and regional championships. Some are popularity contests, others are based on performance. The champion of the New York Racing Association circuit is sometimes held in higher regard than the Eclipse Award winner—especially if you are handicapping an Aqueduct card on a cold January afternoon in Ozone Park.

The Best

In 1985 the best jockey in North America was, depending on which standards were used, Laffitt Pincay (Eclipse Award winner and money leader), Jorge Velasquez (stakes leader), Chris Antley (races leader), or Larry Snyder (winning percentage leader).

Regionally, Randy Romero and Pat Day were the lions of the Midwest; Russell Baze won more races than any other jockey in California; and Richard Migliore unseated Angel Cordero for the New York title.

To illustrate the difficulty in actually singling out the very best, consider the following six lists from the 1985 season, which represent the six most important measurements of riding success:

Money Won		Races Won		Win Percentage	
Pincay	$13,415,049	Antley	469	Snyder	23.6
Velasquez	12,382,914	Romero	416	Day	22.8
McCarron	11,501,308	Day	323	Romero	22.7
Cordero	10,481,672	McCauley	316	Gambardella	22.6

Money Won		Races Won		Win Percentage	
Migliore	7,597,348	Baze	306	Baze	22.4
Day	7,017,986	Gambardella	292	Vargas	21.2
Stevens	6,642,408	Pincay	289	McCarron	21.0
Delahoussaye	6,138,096	McCarron	287	McCauley	20.9
MacBeth	6,134,021	Miller	270	Pincay	20.
Maple	6,051,931	Migliore	266	Cordero	20.3

Stakes Purses		Stakes Wins		1-2-3 Percentage	
Pincay	$8,532,694	Velasquez	57	Gambardella	55.6
Velasquez	7,777,864	McCarron	46	Baze	54.6
McCarron	6,767,918	Cordero	45	Day	54.1
Cordero	6,226,401	Pincay	38	Romero	53.1
Day	3,980,353	Antley	37	Vargas	52.4
MacBeth	3,366,213	Day	34	McCarron	51.6
Maple	3,164,507	Romero	32	Cordero	51.4
Delahoussaye	2,997,349	Delahoussaye	31	Pincay	50.9
Shoemaker	2,950,064	Stevens	28	Enriquez	50.6
Stevens	2,897,533	Shoemaker	26	Snyder	49.1

Only three jockeys made all six lists: Laffit Pincay, Chris McCarron, and Pat Day. So they must be our best all-purpose jockeys, right? Five different riders appeared in the No. 1 spot, with Pincay the only one to lead in two categories. Obviously, based on these tables, the Panamanian powerhouse was the best of the best.

Pincay, however, benefited from a flaw in racing's statistical fabric which hopefully will be mended soon. Beginning in 1982, bonuses ranging from $500,000 to $2,000,000 have been offered for two-, three-, and four-race sweeps. This is a public-relations gimmick of the highest order, fully equipped with a severe statistical bias that can throw a vicious spike into any sensible graph. On top of all that, it is historically unfair. Once the first race in the bonus series was run, only the winner became eligible for the bonus. Furthermore, if the bonus was won, only those principals involved in the final race of the series were credited with the extra cash.

This presented no real problem in 1983 and 1984 when All Along, John Henry, and Slew o'Gold won bonus sweeps. The same owners, trainers, and jockeys were involved every step of the way. But in 1985, when Horse of the Year Spend A Buck banked an extra $2,000,000 by adding the Jersey Derby to victories in the Cherry Hill Mile, Garden State Stakes, and Kentucky Derby, the man in the saddle—*for the first time*—was Laffit Pincay.

Angel Cordero rode Spend A Buck in the first three legs of the bonus series. He tried hard to get out of another commitment on the day of the Jersey Derby, but he failed. (The resourceful Cordero was even willing to helicopter from Belmont Park to Garden State Park if the Jersey Derby post time could be delayed.) So, in effect, Pincay, who rode one of his best races ever, was credited with a $2,000,000 prize that was made possible by the groundwork of another jockey. Without the bonus, Pincay falls to third place on both the money-won list and the stakes purses list of 1985, giving Jorge Velasquez the top spot in three columns instead of just one. Who's No. 1 now?

The Right Questions

Those obsessed with arguing over who's best—McCarron or Cordero or Pincay or one of the many on the local racing scene—will spend their lives in eternal frustration. Instead, wouldn't it be more satisfying to find out what the best do best? Wouldn't it ultimately be more profitable at the betting windows? Even the most successful riders lose nearly five of every six races. The raw data gives us mounts, wins, and a winning percentage. But beyond that, is it possible to know what kind of race a jockey is most likely to win? Would it be profitable if we did know?

The answer to those questions is a resounding *yes*. So let's dig right in. A study group is required, and for this group we will use 10 of the best jockeys of the 1980s. But remember: Even if you never have a chance to bet on Bill Shoemaker or Angel Cordero at your local track, you can use these same principles of measurement to discover a hometown "Cordero" of your very own.

To assemble a fair list of the 10 best jockeys of the '80s, we will turn to the most widely recognized year-end standings, those for money won and races won. The money list has a greater impact simply because the best jockeys win the most money (you can also keep track of this on a local level). Therefore, an appearance among the first 10 on the money lists of the 1980s is given greater weight than races won in coming up with our own top 10.

Enough justification. After all, this list is designed to teach us something about the tendencies of top jockeys, not qualify them for the Racing Hall of Fame. Here are the 10 jockeys we'll study, with a few vital stats thrown in:

Name	Home Base	Birthdate	Ht.	Wt.
Laffit Pincay, Jr.	California	12-29-46	5'2"	117
Chris McCarron	California	3-27-55	5'2"	109
Angel Cordero, Jr.	New York	11- 8-42	5'3"	113
Eddie Delahoussaye	California	9-21-51	5'3"	115
Jorge Velasquez	New York	12-28-46	5'3"	113
Pat Day	Midwest	11-13-53	4'11"	100
Eddie Maple	New York	11- 8-48	5'3"	113
Bill Shoemaker	California	9-19-31	4'11"	95
Patrick Valenzuela	California	10-17-62	5'4"	112
Richard Migliore	New York	3-14-64	5'4"	110

In all, 38 different riders made a top-10 appearance on at least one list between 1980 and 1985. Our Top 10 leaves out a lot of obvious favorites. What about Jose Santos, the young tiger of the New York circuit, or Gary Stevens, his California counterpart? Eclipse Award–winning apprentice Wesley Ward looked like the real thing in 1984. Was he only the victim of a sophomore jinx in a sour '85? Many feel Randy Romero ranks with the best, so why should he be penalized for missing much of 1983–1984 after being severely burned in a freak steambox accident? And, by the end of 1986, Russell Baze, Chris Antley, and Donald Miller may have fled their small ponds to succeed on major circuits.

Points well made. But there are rarely any accidental entries on the yearly top-10 lists. The ground feels quite safe. The tendencies we're looking for can be measured on any level, whether focused on the top 10 at Charles Town midway through the meet or on all jockeys between the ages of 35 and 40. The numbers should work anytime, anywhere.

If He Only Had Wings

Angel Cordero is the man they love to hate. Cordero has probably absorbed more abuse from the New York boo-birds than any rider in history. He and the Big Apple were made for each other. "I've never seen a rider create such tension," said the late Alfred Shelhamer, a California racing official who cringed everytime Cordero hit town.

When Cordero's numbers are considered in an unemotional light, however, he is obviously one of only a handful of jockeys consistently employed by owners and trainers who have a hot horse ready to roll for the big money. Here is his profile:

Category	Mounts	Wins	Win %
Overall	1,150	233	20.3
Short	553	107	19.3
Long	597	126	21.1
$100,000 & up	105	19	18.1
$40,000–$99,999	162	35	21.6
$39,999 & under	358	75	20.9
Fillies	395	71	18.0
Maiden	230	37	16.1
Claiming	295	67	22.7
Turf	287	47	16.4

Cordero is one of only three riders on our list (the others were Pincay and Velasquez) to ride in more than 100 races worth $100,000 or more. His appetite also leans toward longer races, although not to the extreme we will see later with someone like Bill Shoemaker. Besides, Cordero represents the antithesis of the Shoemaker style. He got his nickname, "El Tigre," for his wildman finishes, his daring maneuvers in heavy traffic, and his outright intimidation of other horses and riders. Some observers claim that Cordero terrifies his horses into their best performances.

His statistical trend toward distance races is more sensibly explained by the nature of the sport, not the rider himself. Like most great professional athletes, Cordero rises to the most important occasions. And those occasions in horse racing take place more often in distance events. If the money were loaded in the sprint races, you can bet Cordero would be near the top of that category instead. His blind spots were fillies and maidens, types of horses which usually require patience and finesse. Cordero's forte is aggression.

What does the Cordero profile tell us? He is more likely to ride in—and win—a distance race rather than a sprint. He always shows up for the big money, and his combined winning percentage in races worth $40,000 and up is 20.2 percent. His weaknesses come in turf races and maiden races, both percentages well below his overall winning percentage.

Significantly, 1985 may be the last year representative of Cordero's talents. He was severely injured in a racing spill early in 1986, suffering considerable internal damage. He vowed a successful comeback, and no one doubted his word, especially after he won with the first two horses he rode and then went on to win his eleventh consecutive jockey title at the prestigious Saratoga meeting. Although he came back to ride well the rest of the year, at the age of 44 Cordero's body clock is ticking louder than ever.

Time for the Bigtime

Until *Pat Day* competes full-time in New York or California, his numbers will be muddled by the second-rate circuit he dominates. (Day took shots at both coasts in his youth and failed.) No one doubts he would be a solid success in the major leagues. His increasing forays to New York and Los Angeles for stakes engagements are usually successful. For now, however, Day's lifestyle choice is Midwest all the way. His serene religious attitude leaves no room for anxiety over his ultimate place in history. And so he seems quite satisfied with the kind of business that produces the following profile:

Category	Mounts	Wins	Win %
Overall	1,417	323	22.8
Short	857	200	23.3
Long	660	123	22.0
$100,000 & up	63	13	20.6
$40,000–$99,999	45	11	24.4
$39,999 & under	420	108	25.7
Fillies	582	139	23.9
Maiden	338	63	18.6
Claiming	551	128	23.2
Turf	154	21	13.6

Start by throwing out that turf figure. In 1985, Day won most of his races at Oaklawn Park in Hot Springs, Arkansas, and Churchill Downs in Louisville, Kentucky. Neither track had a turf course, a painfully obvious limitation when measuring grass racing.

Day's circuit does not provide him with tremendous purse opportunities or particularly good horses to ride. As a result, Day's entire scale is tilted toward the weak end—claimers and Quality C events. Put him in New York and his claiming win totals would probably drop while his Class C and B totals would increase, simply because the emphasis in the big city is on a better grade of animal. Day rides a representative percentage of filly winners and maiden winners, figures that probably would not change in New York or California.

A figure sure to change if Day went bigtime would be the sprint/route distribution. The cheap, sore horses Day must deal with are protected by shorter races (less wear and tear). Sprints are very stressful on extremely fast horses; but claimers run at basically the same pace, never going faster than they absolutely have to. Day's record is overloaded with sprints because of opportunity, not ability.

Other than the turf figure, the Day profile is an admirably consistent one. Note his healthy percentage of winners in $100,000-plus events. This is especially significant, since he usually has had to travel far and wide to find such opportunities, then adapt quickly to overnight changes in racing surface, weather, and opposition.

In 1986, Day did his 1985 performance a notch better. His overall winning percentage flirted with the 30 percent mark, roughly the equivalent of batting .400. Still, Day was doing it in the sub-major leagues. Hitting .400 in Triple A is a notable achievement, but when you do it in New York or L.A. you can own the franchise.

The Ragin' Cajun

The knock on *Eddie Delahoussaye* out West is that the man from Louisiana only gets psyched up for the big ones and lets a lot of the little races slide. Let's check that out, based on the tendencies displayed in 1985:

Category	Mounts	Wins	Win %
Overall	1,216	174	14.3
Short	644	92	14.3
Long	572	81	14.3
$100,000 & up	70	8	11.4
$40,000–$99,999	137	28	20.4
$39,999 & under	254	38	15.0
Fillies	456	71	15.6
Maiden	333	43	12.9
Claiming	422	57	13.5
Turf	272	31	11.2

Delahoussaye was not prolific in the top races on the California circuit, where he competed head to head with Pincay, McCarron, Valenzuela, and Shoemaker. At the next level, however, he excelled. His winning percentage in $40,000-to-$99,999 races far outranked anything else in his profile, including his overall percentage. And even his figure in the $39,999 and under column exceeds his overall figure.

Both his maiden and claiming figures were below his average, though, leading us to believe that he may prefer to ride the better quality horses. In explaining the challenges of riding claimers and maidens, Delahoussaye can tell us why they might not be much fun to get along with.

"Some young horses come out acting like an old horse," said Delahoussaye, who rides regularly for such trainers as Neil Drysdale, Gary Jones, and Richard Mulhall, all of them good with young horses. "Nothing bothers them. Not the starting gate, not getting bumped around, not getting sand thrown in their face. But those are the exceptions.

"No matter how good they are, a maiden can be very unpredictable. I've been banged around by 2-year-olds in the morning, but I've never been hurt on one in the afternoon—knock on wood. Without any experience they might jump the fence the first time they see the whip, or get bumped by another horse. I'm a little more reluctant to use the stick with a young horse. I don't like surprises."

As for claimers, Delahoussaye had a tip for the handicappers.

"A horse that's been a claimer all his life, you can't do anything to change his style of running," said the jockey. "But an old class horse—a horse dropping down from stakes or allowances to run for a claiming tag—sometimes you can change his way of going. I've seen it happen many times."

So, if a claiming race sets up well for an early speed horse, an entrant with a trace of class in his past might be able to take advantage of the situation?

"That's right," Delahoussaye replied. "You might be able to put an old class horse on the lead when he's been coming from behind, or take him back when he's been going to the lead. They're smart old horses, even though they are cheap now. They remember what to do if you remind them."

Straight-Shooter

Doesn't matter if you want incisive analysis or a wisecrack—*Eddie Maple* is your man. After a miserable showing in the 1984 Breeders' Cup Distaff aboard the well-regarded Miss Oceana, Maple just shook his head and said, "Well, they taught this filly how to rate, but they forgot to teach her how to finish." Later that same day Maple watched helplessly from atop Track Barron as his former mount, Wild Again, won the Breeders' Cup Classic. Alluding to the gross misjudgment that cost him the mount, Maple said, "I believe that's the first time a jockey agent ever took off the winner of a $3,000,000 race." It was, of course, the first $3,000,000 race in history. Here is the 1985 version of Eddie Maple:

Category	Mounts	Wins	Win %
Overall	1,242	152	12.3
Short	616	63	10.2
Long	626	90	14.4
$100,000 & up	79	9	11.4
$40,000–$99,999	98	10	10.2
$39,999 & under	395	65	16.5
Fillies	505	69	13.7
Maiden	350	41	11.7
Claiming	320	28	8.6
Turf	287	44	15.3

Maple does his most consistent winning in the $39,999 and under category, which includes allowance races just a cut below the best of that bunch. Based upon these figures—and the nature of Maple's overall business profile—it would not appear profitable to follow him in claiming races. Much of his riding is done for a handful of trainers who trust him with their unproven, well-bred, and expensive young horses. Maple spends many afternoons "test driving" a variety of horsepower.

The most dramatic tendency displayed by Maple is his affinity for distance races over short races. The 4.2 percent swing in success rate is the highest (with Shoemaker) among the entire group of 10 we are studying. When asked about this aspect of his profile, Maple offered a good explanation:

"You never know how things like that get started," Maple said. "I like to think I have a little natural ability when it comes to riding routes. But you've still got to have the horse.

"In 1971 I lost the mount on a nice colt named Gleaming to Braulio Baeza for the Lawrence Realization, a mile and five-eighths grass race. I ended up on a little bitty filly named Specious, no bigger than my dog. Took her back to last and came running to beat Gleaming and pay about $60."

Since then, Maple has won practically every major New York race beyond 10 furlongs at least once, including the Belmont Stakes (1980 and 1985), Suburban Handicap ('76, '77), Travers Stakes ('80, '81), Alabama Stakes ('76, '81), Jockey Club Gold Cup, Man o'War Stakes, and Sword Dancer Handicap. Maple was the last man to ride Secretariat when "Big Red" sang his swan song with a 1⅝-mile course record in the 1973 Canadian International Championship at Woodbine.

"On one hand, a race gets more complicated as it goes longer," Maple said. "I'd say that it's true a jockey makes more difference to the outcome of a route race than he does in a sprint. On the other hand, there is more time for things to sort themselves out going long, if you have the patience to let it happen.

"In a race, say, like the Belmont Stakes, for the first half-mile I'm riding my race, my plan. After about a half-mile, though, I let the horse tell me what to do. It's my job to get him into a position where he can get the job done. There's just as many chances to get into trouble going long as there is in a sprint. They run a lot of mile and a quarter races on the turf at Belmont, and if you're caught inside horses going nowhere around that first turn, that's it. You're stuck. I'd have to get off that horse and tell the trainer, 'Well, we only got stopped once, but it was for five-eighths of a mile.'

"If I was a betting man, I think I'd do pretty well handicapping route races. In a 10-horse field I could throw out 5 right away just because they don't have the stamina or the breeding. Natural speed is important, although not necessarily front-running kind of speed. I also think it helps for a jockey to have ridden the horse before.

"I rode a $35,000 claimer for Joe Cantey for the first time the other day. He pulled me to the lead with about three-eighths to go and I thought there was no way we could lose. He finished a bad third. So when I rode him back I knew I had to do something different. That's my job. He was in against the same horses, other than the winner. I took him back, and then back a little more, and we were maybe 11 lengths off the lead at the five-eighths. Turning for home I took him out and came running, and he won for fun. But it took me that first ride to know what the horse needed."

Some handicappers refuse to touch a filly race. "Unreliable" is the claim. "Subject to the whims of hormones" say others. "Never bet them until spring is over" is the warning. Since roughly 40 percent of all races are restricted to females, jockeys do not have the same choice. Indeed, some of the best riders are especially handy with fillies and mares. Maple boasts solid contacts with trainers whose clients are successful breeders, thus providing for a steady stream of well-bred fillies. (Many commercial breeders tend to sell their colts and race their fillies.) With 45 percent of his winners coming in filly races, Maple can be called a specialist in this field. He should be. He works hard at it.

"From the day I started riding I understood that fillies were different from colts," Maple said. "More so than with colts, you've got to get inside a filly's head. Really figure out what she's thinking and decide what makes her happiest. It doesn't really have anything to do with using or not using the stick. Some fillies respond to the whip better than colts. A filly's not happy, she doesn't run for you. That's where's they're different from colts.

"An example. I'm on a filly and we are lead up to the pony for the post parade. Right away I can tell my filly is agitated by something. I tell the pony rider to stay clear, don't touch her. In two steps my filly is happy, and she runs her race.

"I'll pay more attention to who gets on fillies in the morning. I'll watch how they handle them and maybe pick up a few things that will help me in the afternoon. It all adds up. The most important thing is sensitivity, and I like to think I'm very sensitive to what they are feeling. Treat them different because they are different."

Two of a Kind . . . Kind of

So far we have not compared jockeys—that's not the point we're trying to make. Each rider has his own statistical personality, and that personality can be used by the handicapper to decide if the jockey is right for a particular race.

Indulge your author, however, in a direct comparison of the men who were kings of West Coast racing for the first half of the 1980s: *Laffit Pincay* and *Chris McCarron*. Their 1985 profiles follow:

CHRIS MCCARRON

Category	Mounts	Wins	Win %
Overall	1,367	287	21.0
Short	683	136	19.9
Long	684	151	22.1
$100,000 & up	88	21	23.9
$40,000–$99,999	166	33	19.9
$39,999 & under	302	71	23.5
Fillies	518	119	23.0
Maiden	359	76	21.2
Claiming	452	86	19.0
Turf	313	71	22.7

LAFFIT PINCAY

Category	Mounts	Wins	Win %
Overall	1,409	289	20.5
Short	737	146	19.8
Long	672	143	21.3
$100,000 & up	84	20	23.8
$40,000–$99,999	151	34	22.5

Category	Mounts	Wins	Win %
$39,999 & under	306	73	23.9
Fillies	509	98	19.3
Maiden	373	72	19.3
Claiming	495	90	18.2
Turf	286	52	18.2

Right down the line, Pincay's and McCarron's winning percentages are tantalizingly close. Most of the categories harbor differences of less than two percentage points. There are two columns, however, where the champions take separate paths—those of turf races and filly races. The figures for '85 would seem to justify the temptation to bet on McCarron over Pincay in both situations.

The turf disparity is hard to explain. Pincay certainly has no weaknesses when it comes to riding on the grass. A look at his victories aboard Perrault in the 1982 Arlington Million or Erin's Isle in the 1983 San Juan Capistrano Handicap quiets that argument. The filly difference, however, makes sense. Pincay's greatest successes with female runners has usually come with the big, robust, almost studdish mares, who are in the minority among physical types. They respond to the kind of strength supplied by Pincay, who Dr. Robert Kerlan (of the Los Angeles Rams and Lakers) called "pound for pound the best-built athlete I've ever seen." Adored, a star of 1985, is a good example of a big mare who ran well for Pincay. So is Susan's Girl, champion of the early 1970s.

Except for an occasional eccentric lapse of memory (he once missed a mount when he let a cabbie take him to the wrong San Francisco racetrack), Pincay refuses to age like a normal athlete. A California racing official once noted that the older, more successful jockeys will sometimes steer clear of undue risk when the purse is not of sufficient inspiration. "Not Laffit," he quickly added. "He is in a class by himself. You will never see him give a sanitized ride, no matter what the situation."

Through the first six years of the decade, the Pincay and McCarron camps were deadlocked over the relative merits of their heroes. If McCarron did not win a southern California title, then Pincay did. (Only Delahoussaye, at Santa Anita in 1982, and Sandy Hawley at the Oak Tree meeting of 1980, interrupted their dominance between 1980 and 1985.) In 1983 McCarron won the riding title at every major meeting in southern California. In 1984 Pincay took back the prestigious Santa Anita crown. After McCarron caught his breath he won the rest.

McCarron's few critics cite him for being too smart for his own good. His ability to monitor the opposition is unparalleled, but some believe it works against him. "I've seen him overthink a race and get beat," said one West Coast trainer. "He'll be riding more than just his own horse. He rides more from the gut now than he used to, though."

From 1980 through the halfway point of the 1986 season, Chris McCarron's mounts earned more money than any rider in the world. Over those 6½ years, horses ridden by the redhead raked in $62,476,684, compared to $61,037,574 for Laffit Pincay. (Angel Cordero, with $57.7 million, was sidelined for most of the first half of '86 with injuries.)

McCarron still has a ways to go to reach Pincay's record total in the all-time money category, however. In 1985 Pincay caught and passed Shoemaker, who had been the leader since 1964. Pincay began the 1986 season with a career total of more than $106,000,000 in purses banked by his mounts.

So you would think that by now such champions would be comfortable with the pressure of riding for major money in world-class races. Think again.

The toughest position for any athlete is probably the spotlight . . . before the event. The Las Vegas favorite in a title fight, the people's choice for the Super Bowl, even the hometown hero in a downhill slalom each have the same problem—no excuses.

McCarron recalled the most pressure he ever felt before a race.

"It was the 1984 Arlington Million," he said. "John Henry had never been better. I can't remember ever having more confidence in a horse than I did in him for that race. At the same time, I was never more nervous, because the only way he was going to lose is if I lost it, not him." He won.

Pincay tells a similar story, revolving around his historic date with Spend a Buck and a potential $2.6 million payday in the 1985 Jersey Derby.

"I ate good the night before the race," he said. "Like I was getting ready for a fight. I thought I was on the best horse no matter what. At the same time, I wanted to ride the horse the way his people wanted me to ride. If he got beat, I didn't want there to be any excuses from me. But I really didn't see any way he could get beat. That's why I had a lot of pressure on me. When you don't see a way out . . ."

And sometimes the pressures placed upon athletes in a gambling game are too hideous to even consider.

A successful young trainer once lost a race and then heard later that a man had been financially ruined by gambling on the horse. The trainer took it to heart, depressed at the thought that even by the most indirect route he could affect a person's life so badly. Shoemaker, who had been the rider, took the trainer aside and told him a story.

"I lost a tough photo-finish on a favorite one day," Shoemaker recalled. "The boo-birds were really out to get me. That doesn't bother me much. They pay their money and they can let off a little steam if they want. Then the next day the news was spreading all over the track. Some guy had bet a lot of money on the horse I rode, and I guess it was all he had. He went out to his car in the track parking lot and shot himself dead. It bothered me, sure. Bothered me a lot. But if I let something like that really get to me, how can I ever ride again?"

Lost in the Flood

Richard Migliore, the native New Yorker who was born in 1964, has youth on his side in his battle with the likes of Cordero, Velasquez, Maple, and now Jose Santos and Randy Romero. You would think that with all this competition there wouldn't be much left for even a talented young rider like Migliore. Here's what he got in 1985:

Category	Mounts	Wins	Win %
Overall	1,666	266	16.0
Short	876	140	16.0
Long	790	126	16.0
$100,000 & up	59	6	10.2
$40,000–$99,999	139	27	19.4
$39,999 & under	500	77	15.4
Fillies	662	104	15.7
Maiden	442	59	13.3
Claiming	526	97	18.4
Turf	241	37	15.4

Migliore suffered the traditional post-apprentice slump in 1982 and '83 after his Eclipse Award-winning 1981 campaign. In 1984 he rebounded, and in 1985 he was back in a confident groove, displaying a seasoned maturity and riding such high-profile horses as Win and Eternal Prince. Yet he still seems to get the leftovers when it comes to the major horses and the top stakes events. He was further challenged in 1986 when his home turf was invaded by Santos and Romero.

Migliore made the most of his opportunities in the $40,000-to-$99,999 races, many of them weekday features and small stakes. He was also a prolific winner of claiming races, although that's not the sort of reputation you want to get if stardom is on your mind.

The only real downward spike on the Migliore graph is in the $100,000-plus events, the cream of the racing cupboard. Only 3.5 percent of his total activity for 1985 came in the big money games. His winning percentage of 10.2 obviously suffered from lack of opportunity. But then, how many job-seekers have been confronted with, "We can't hire you without the experience."

Until he gets that experience, Migliore's steady hand in all other categories will serve him well. Fortunately, the $100,000-and-up races represent a small percentage of the handicapping situations faced by the bettor. A Migliorean profile, with its relatively even complexion, instills confidence despite the lack of big-race wins.

Doing It His Way

Bill Shoemaker, the elder statesman of the jockey fraternity, has a right to specialize, but this is ridiculous! A staggering 66 percent of his winners came in races at a mile or more. (Maple is second in this category with 59 percent, followed by Cordero at 54 percent and McCarron at 53 percent.) Here are Shoemaker's numbers for 1985:

Category	Mounts	Wins	Win %
Overall	721	80	11.1
Short	311	27	8.7
Long	410	53	12.9
$100,000 & up	73	10	13.7
$40,000–$99,999	111	17	15.3
$39,999 & under	183	22	12.0
Fillies	290	36	12.4
Maiden	175	18	10.3
Claiming	179	13	7.3
Turf	239	27	11.3

The numbers further suggest that if every race were worth $50,000 or more and run over a distance of ground, Shoemaker would still be at the top of the heap. Given this record for 1985, when Shoemaker turned 54, the sports world should not have been so shocked the following spring when the little Texan won the biggest Class A distance race of them all, the Kentucky Derby.

Shoemaker is the specialist when it comes to winning distance races with significant money attached, when patience and a keen sense of the passage of time are priceless assests. Shoemaker's prejudice toward distance races is hardly surprising. The man has become a multimillionaire through his ability to nurse a horse along, quietly, without fuss, and save the best for last. The longer the race, the more this kind of style pays off. Riders in too much of a hurry are soon unemployed when distance events are carded. Shoemaker is always in demand. It also should be noted that sprint races are a young man's game, especially in the American style of racing, where the first 3 furlongs are run much faster than the last 3.

Given the right mount, Shoemaker's skills can still transcend his age. Just don't ask him to beat and hustle that extra step of speed out of a sore old claimer in a $15,000 weekday race at Hollywood Park. Chris McCarron once said the trick to riding was interfering with the horse as little as possible. "Shoemaker is the epitome of that philosophy," McCarron pointed out. "He sits still while other jocks are busy. He makes the horse think he's running free. And he has found that spot on the horse's neck where he can set his hands and make the horse feel the most comfortable on the bit. I'm still looking for that spot."

If you were to hide the identity of the Shoemaker table and give it to a handicapper, chances are he would probably file it under "Desperate Bets Only" and go on to the next entry. If you were to tell him that the profile represented the work of a 54-year-old jockey who accepts only about 800 mounts a year, he would not be the least bit surprised.

Then, if you told him that the same jockey banked more than $11,000,000 in purses in 1985 and '86, the handicapper would fix you with a cold stare and reply, "Must be Shoemaker."

The point being that Shoemaker—and steady veterans like him—can never be counted out when the game plays to their strengths. There are senior jockeys all over the country who continue to win when the circumstances are right. Handicappers risk making an expensive mistake when they fail to recognize those opportunities.

Power Forward

Patrick Valenzuela is the kind of man you want on a cheap horse in a sprint race. Valenzuela's ability to gain ground at the start of the race and hold on until the end is without equal. And the fact that he does it in California, where early speed is an obsession, is even more impressive. Just look at his dramatic tendencies in 1985:

Category	Mounts	Wins	Win %
Overall	1,281	197	15.4
Short	746	123	16.5
Long	535	74	13.8
$100,000 & up	48	8	16.7
$40,000–99,999	92	14	15.2
$39,999 & under	223	33	14.8
Fillies	505	82	16.2
Maiden	374	48	12.8
Claiming	544	94	17.3
Turf	181	18	9.9

Valenzuela rides far more sprints than routes and wins them more often. In fact, 62 percent of his winners came in sprint races in 1985. Trainers know it, owners know it, and the public knows it. Valenzuela possesses a remarkable ability to push a horse away from the starting gate as soon as the stall doors spring open. Perched on his tiptoes, braced for the sudden thrust of acceleration, his balance is uncanny as he goes from zero to 38 m.p.h. in less than 40 yards. He rarely loses those valuable few steps at the beginning of a sprint, which can translate into a narrow loss less than 90 seconds later.

That's the good news. The bad news could be that Valenzuela excels at sprint races because his skills at distance races are limited. A dumb assumption, on the face of it, since he could hardly be counted among the top 10 of the 1980s while burdened with such an expensive weakness.

Still, it is apparent that when Valenzuela wins it will be in a sprint race more often than not.

"How you get out of the gate determines how good a rider you are in sprints," said Valenzuela, who got his early training on the sagebrush circuit of New Mexico. "Horses are trained to react when a jockey moves on them in the gate, so you've got to relax and just sit there like a bump on a log. A horse is so keyed up in the gate that anything can set them off. I once had a horse flip over backwards and pin me against the back doors. He's crushing me, I'm yelling for help, and at the same time I'm praying the doors don't open. If they do, I'm on the ground and the horse is on top of me.

"So you relax, you try to get the horse's feet under him and set right, and you listen for everything to get quiet. That usually means it's time to go. I stare at the front doors, and as soon as I see them open a crack I scream at my horse and push him out of there. I'm not really trying to beat the gate. But after riding a lot of races you get a sense of timing, being able to see the doors start to open."

Essentially, Valenzuela—or any top gate rider—can recognize *the beginning* of a split second and seize that advantage at the break. The stretching of time is an ability shared by the best athletes. Jackie Stewart, the Formula I racecar champion, described events at 180-m.p.h. in his autobiographical journal *Faster*:

"Everything is clear, neither hurried nor distorted, a tableau spread out in front of you, things going past, a new field coming into view, all of it in sequence, like a slowed-down movie film."

Once away from the gate, Valenzuela's powerful arms and shoulders take over. Picture the upper body of an Olympic swimmer on a pair of spindly legs.

"My dad and uncles, all of them riders, taught me that you use the top of your body to push the horse," Valenzuela said. "You keep your butt still and use your legs for balance.

"Physically, a short race is as demanding as a long one," Valenzuela added. "Oh, your legs might get a little more tired over a route. But in a sprint you ride so much faster, with so much energy and intensity, that you can run out of breath a lot sooner."

Valenzuela would like to be known someday as an all-around rider. He has yet to master the turf, which is inexcusable considering that he rides year-round on turf courses in California. But he has no serious critics when it comes to riding distance races on the main track. Through the 1986 season, Valenzuela remained one of only five jockeys to win the Big Four events at Santa Anita Park: the Charles H. Strub Stakes, the Santa Anita Handicap, the Santa Anita Derby, and the San Juan Capistrano Handicap. The other four are named Shoemaker, Arcaro, Longden, and Pincay.

The Man Has Style

Set a glass of water on this man's back and he won't spill a drop. *Jorge Velasquez* has been a model jockey when it comes to grace under fire. His profile for 1985 shows remarkable consistency in the trenches—the right kind of peaks and very few valleys:

Category	Mounts	Wins	Win %
Overall	1,465	258	17.6
Short	727	127	17.5
Long	738	131	17.7
$100,000 & up	107	19	17.8
$40,000–$99,999	181	46	25.4
$39,999 & under	442	83	18.8
Fillies	588	112	19.0
Maiden	370	55	14.9
Claiming	364	55	15.1
Turf	313	42	13.4

Velasquez maintained a blissful equilibrium between the winning of sprint and route races. That is rare among the veteran riders, who tend to lean toward distance events (see Cordero, Shoemaker, and Pincay). The only renegade number in his '85 profile came in the turf column, with a surprisingly low 13.4 winning percentage while riding primarily in New York, where 15 percent to 20 percent of all races are run on the grass. Why the discrepancy?

The answer: D. Wayne Lukas. Velasquez hooked up with the Lukas New York division in 1985 and virtually ran the table. He broke Lukas maidens and won with Lukas allowance horses. Of Velasquez's 57 stakes victories, 29 of them came aboard Lukas horses. The only problem was that Lukas had no grass horses. Lukas won only four grass races all year in New York (three with the same horse)—and Velasquez rode all four winners. Velasquez was locked into the Lukas stable and missed opportunities he normally would have seized. He was no better or worse on the turf than in previous years. He was simply winning main track races at a far greater rate because of his Lukas connection, and the slice of the pie left for his grass totals was considerably less. Even if you take away those 29 Lukas-trained stakes winners from Velasquez' quality figure, more than half of his wins are still quality races.

Velasquez parlayed his American reputation into a choice riding contract in France for the 1987 season—and will be riding exclusively on grass. Anyway, Fernando Toro has called Jorge Velasquez "the best turf rider in New York." Toro ought to know. He is considered among the very best who ever lived.

Bull Market

A North American racetrack without a turf course these days is a rogue, an outcast, and missing a lot of fun. In the mid-1980s, turf courses were added inside the dirt ovals at Churchill Downs and Keeneland. Such new emporiums as Canterbury Downs and Garden State Park were built with turf racing in mind.

The heavy influx of European race horses—a phenomenon of the last decade—has put a premium upon turf racing in the United States. Major racetracks card as many as three or four turf races a day when the weather permits.

If you have a grass course at your local track, it would be wise to keep separate statistics for turf racing. And if you can find a local rider like Fernando Toro, your future may be secure.

During the Hollywood Park meeting of 1970, Toro won the hearts and wallets of West Coast racing fans with a record total of 46 victories on the grass. The cry in the grandstand became "Viva Bull!" and "Toro! Toro! Toro!," while handicappers added the new "Toro-on-the-turf" factor to their daily equations.

It was not a fluke season for the native of Santiago, Chile. In 1975 he won 75 races during the Hollywood meet—28 of them on the turf. In 1976 he won 40 on the turf. Neither has age blunted his skills. In November of 1983, two months shy of his forty-third birthday, Toro won both divisions of the Hollywood Derby at a mile and one-eighth. One year later he captured the very first Breeders' Cup grass race, winning the $1,000,000 Breeders' Cup Mile with Royal Heroine at (where else?) Hollywood Park. In 1985 Toro orchestrated the surprise of the summer when he won the Sunset Handicap aboard Kings Island, while at the same time beating Hollywood Gold Cup winner Greinton out of a million-dollar bonus. And the 1986 season was no different. Toro won the Budweiser Million aboard the mare Estrapade before a network television audience.

Toro has a few tricks to winning on the grass. But for the most part his riding is reflexive, born of nearly three decades establishing a highly specialized muscle memory that can be activated in a split second. On the ground, however, he is analytical about his craft. What follows is a lesson in turf racing from Professor Toro:

"On the dirt it's go, go, go right from the start. Almost every race comes up the same way. On the turf, no two races are alike. There is a lot of instinct involved. The jockey is more important on the grass than he is on the dirt. Your timing has to be perfect. You have to use your judgment every step of the way. If there is a slow pace, and I'm on a horse without early speed, I have to be prepared for any chance to save even a little bit of ground, always improve my position. If my horse is on the turf for the first time and he's looking around at the people in the infield, or the tote board, I try to get his mind off those things, get him right beside another horse.

"A young rider will have trouble with the turf," Toro said. "He is used to working horses on the dirt only, and he is not ready for the way a horse feels on the turf. Very different. They feel like they are flying, hardly touching the ground. They love the way they are running, and they get more aggressive. Then they go too fast, which is why it is more difficult to judge the pace on the grass."

Handicappers are faced with the same challenges as jockeys are when it comes to anticipating the dynamics of a grass race. Toro was asked to recall a memorable case of unpredictability in a turf race and how he coped. He had a ready reply.

"I look back at a lot of the big races I have won on the turf, and there are many I could have ridden even better. But there was one—I've got the picture hanging on my wall—that was the toughest race I'd ever encountered. It was the American Handicap of 1975 at Hollywood Park. I was on a horse named Montmarte, a nice horse, but there were some really top horses in against us—Ancient Title, Stardust Mel, Top Crowd.

"There was all the speed in the world. Montmarte came from behind anyway, so that really didn't matter. I figured I would just wait and maybe get lucky. So what happens? Bang! First jump out of the gate I'm half a length in front. Then my horse got brave and started pulling. I dropped over from my number eight post position, waiting for somebody else to go on. There was nobody coming. I was in a gallop! We went the first half in 51 seconds. Then I knew what happened. Everyone else in the race was afraid of so much early speed that they all took back!

"Okay. So I know that when they finally come at me they will be flying. I decide I have to move before the others do. Going into the turn my horse changed leads and I opened up. They never caught me. Almost the same thing happened with Kings Island against Greinton."

What a piece of work that was. In the '85 Sunset Handicap, Toro was setting a slow pace with Kings Island, who was carrying six pounds less than the heavily favored Greinton. With a half mile of the mile and one-half race left to run, Toro devised a daring trap and sprung it to perfection. The victim was no less than Laffit Pincay.

"I know Greinton has a big quarter mile run, not much more," Toro recalled. "I want him to use it early, so he is not as strong at the end. So I decide to make my horse run hard the last three-eighths of a mile. Now, Kings Island was a lazy horse, so in order to get him running by the three-eighths pole I had to start working on him at the half-mile pole. Pincay looked over at me, saw that I was asking my horse, so he starts riding Greinton. Only thing is, Greinton has instant acceleration. He has started his run a quarter mile earlier than usual, and he didn't have as much left at the end. I knew I had him all through the stretch.

"The thing about turf races is that there is no perfect way to ride them. Jockeys who think there is lose a lot of races that way. Chris McCarron used to be like that, worrying about every other horse in the race. If he was laying second and the favorite was behind him, he might forget about the horse on the lead and just watch for the favorite because that is what he is expected to do. So what happens? The favorite doesn't run his race and the horse on the lead gets away and wins. On the turf, you can never be afraid to do the unexpected."

Class dismissed.

Chris Craft—The Seagram's Award

In 1975, Seagram Distillers Co. began awarding $10,000 checks to the top athletes in 10 different sports categories. Horse racing or, more accurately, jockeys, was one of them. The winners were determined by computer tallies based on programs developed by the Elias Sports Bureau, well known for its statistical work in baseball, football, and basketball.

Horse racing, however, was a brave new world for the Elias people.

"When Jorge Tejeira turned out to be the winner in 1976, we knew the system needed some refinements," said the Bureau's Peter Hirdt. "Don't get me wrong. Tejeira was a fine rider and had a great season, mostly kicking behind at Keystone Park and old Liberty Bell. Essentially, what we needed to do was net out the effect of the more insignificant races."

No one in their right mind called Tejeira the best rider of 1976. Not when Laffit Pincay, Angel Cordero, Jorge Velasquez, Sandy Hawley, and Jacinto Vasquez were at the height of their powers. But how can a system be taken seriously if its results can be shouted down by public perceptions?

"In a perfect world, we develop the system and then do 10,000 simulations," Hirdt replied. "It is virtually impossible to get a young system going right from the start, especially one in which you have a result only once a year. We had an analogous situation in baseball one year when it was obvious Ron Guidry and Jim Rice had seasons that were head and shoulders above the competition. When the final stats did not reflect that, we did some off-season refining to make sure the most important statistical categories were given the proper weight.

"At the same time, everyone knows that racing is not an equal opportunity sport," Hirdt added. "Because of their reputations, jockeys like McCarron, Pincay, and Cordero will always be given better horses to ride simply because of who they are. That gives them an edge going in."

A synopsis of the Elias jockey program states:

"Since pressure builds and the competitive challenge increases in proportion to the prestige and distance of a race, the Seagram computer performs a comprehensive analysis of each jockey's performance emphasizing longer, richer races. The longer the race, the greater the demand for a rider to exhibit his overall riding skill: a sense of pace and timing, general race strategy, and physical stamina.

"Thus, a winning ride in a $50,000 event at a mile and a quarter would be of greater value than a $75,000 race at 6 furlongs. Similarly, as a race's purse value increases, so does its mathematical weight. The emphasis on quality races minimizes the value of races at smaller tracks with low competitive ratings, and separates riders of lesser skill from those competing at the nation's leading tracks."

By the 1980s, the system had become highly sophisticated. It had also become virtually a one-man show. Five different jockeys won the first five awards: Bill Shoemaker (1975), Jorge Tejeira (1976), Steve Cauthen (1977), Darrel McHargue (1978), and Laffit Pincay (1979). Then the Chris McCarron era began.

The freckle-faced redhead from Dorchester, Massachusetts, won the prize in 1980, '81, '83, '84, and '85, interrupted only by Angel Cordero in 1982. During the same period of time McCarron topped the national money list only twice and the wins list just once. Obviously, Seagram was measuring something else.

"Everyone figures Velasquez was a cinch to win in 1985 because of all the stakes races (57) he won," Hirdt said. "Never mind that a large percentage of those were for one trainer, Wayne Lukas. The system is set up to detect just such a pattern, however. More points will be earned by a jockey who wins 10 stakes on 10 different horses at five different tracks than the jockey who wins 10 stakes on two horses at the same track.''

Seagram scaled back its awards program in 1986, eliminating, among others, the jockey category. Seems the company was not getting enough publicity mileage for its 10 grand. In the rubble of numbers left behind, however, were 11 years' worth of solid work.

"I like to think it was consistency," McCarron said shortly after receiving his final award. "That's what I strive for. When they asked me if I'd mind flying to New York to get the '85 award I told them, 'Hell, no! I'll go anywhere to pick up a check for $10,000.' Am I disappointed the award was ended? You could say that, yes.''

The top five jockeys, 1980–1885, according to Seagram's performance points, were as follows:

1980	1981	1982
McCarron	McCarron	Cordero
Cordero	Pincay	Pincay
Pincay	Cordero	McCarron
Fell	Delahoussaye	Velasquez
Velasquez	Hawley	Delahoussaye

1983	1984	1985
McCarron	McCarron	McCarron
Cordero	Pincay	Velasquez
Pincay	Cordero	Pincay
Day	Day	Cordero
Velasquez	Velasquez	Day

It looks like an exclusive club, with the same five or six guys cutting up all the spoils. Bear in mind, however, that the $10,000 was winner-take-all. There was no second prize. And the riders were kept in suspense until the computer finished its work and checked its facts after each season ended on December 31.

In 1985, McCarron topped none of the traditional riding categories. Yet, because the competition measured overall consistency under daily pressure, he still held out hope for the Seagram title. When the call came in January, McCarron was told he had won the closest race in the history of the award—.35 of a point ahead of Velasquez and .41 ahead of Laffit Pincay.

"There might have been one rainy, cold day somewhere along the way," said McCarron, "when I was lying in bed with a miserable cold, wishing I didn't have seven mounts that afternoon. And I rode anyway, and won maybe a race or two. That day might have been the difference in winning the $10,000."

No one has been able to place a precise value upon the contribution of the jockey to the performance of the horse. Hairbrained theories give figures that range from 5 percent to 25 percent. Basically, it is a waste of time to worry about something that can't be accurately quantified.

It is important, however, to be able to tell which jockeys will be able to contribute more to the performance of a given horse in a given race than others. The Elias methods tackled that question, looking for consistent performance in the most challenging circumstances. Individual handicappers must arrive at their own conclusions. The most important factor in sorting out jockeys is to be true to your own needs. Make sure that the talents you measure or identify are relevant to the races you are betting. The tendency you're searching for may be the best rider from the gate, on the turf, or in a claimer.

Remember, the best jockey is the one who wins . . . for *you*. Let history worry about the champions.

Peer Pressure

During the summer of 1981, *San Diego Tribune* sportswriter Jerry Froide polled 16 jockeys in the local Del Mar colony. Promising anonymity, Froide asked them to pick the best of their peers in several categories of riding skills. The results say a lot about perceptions from the inside.

On the day the poll was published, the top 10 in the Del Mar jockey standings were Chris McCarron, Eddie Delahoussaye, Laffit Pincay, Sandy Hawley, Bill Shoemaker, Darrel McHargue, Marco Castaneda, Patrick Valenzuela, Bill Winland (apprentice), and, tied for tenth, Frank Olivares and Fernando Toro.

McCarron was on his way to a record $8,397,604 in purses that season. Pincay would also break the old record (*his* old record) with a final total of $7,918,189 by year's end. Shoemaker had just turned 50 and was riding high as the new partner of a 6-year-old gelding named John Henry, the eventual Horse of the Year. Hawley was hot after a good meeting at Hollywood Park, and Valenzuela was the star on the rise.

The voting went like this:

Best at judging the pace—Shoemaker (10½ votes), Delahoussaye (1½).

Best come-from-behind rider—McCarron (4), Shoemaker (3), Delahoussaye (3).

Strongest hand rider—Pincay (14½), McCarron (1).

Best whip rider—Hawley (5), McCarron (5).

Best out of the gate—Valenzuela (3), Terry Lipham (3).

Best on the lead—Valenzuela (4), McCarron (3).

Best grass rider—Toro (12), four tied with one vote.

Most improved rider—Delahoussaye (4), Valenzuela (4).

Best all-around rider—Pincay (6), Shoemaker (4), McCarron (4).

Eddie Delahoussaye, a national champion while riding in the Midwest in 1977, took exception to the fact that he was an "improved" rider. "I don't think I've improved as much as I've just altered my style to suit California," he told the *Tribune*.

Shoemaker complimented his associates on their consensus in the pace category. "They made an excellent choice," he joked. "Actually, it's something you gain with experience. You've got to go around and around that track plenty of times to develop your judgment of pace."

As far as the selection of Pincay as the best all-around, it was certainly no surprise. Fellow riders appreciate Pincay on a much different level than the betting public, however. They are first-hand witnesses to his daily struggle with weight. The man can afford almost anything he wishes, as long as it has nothing to do with food. Chris McCarron watched Pincay chew and spit out a nut bar one day, then turned to his personal ice chest and fished out a Cherry Coke, grabbed a handful of Cheetos, and shook his head. "The man is amazing," McCarron said. "I don't think I could live like that. I'm not sure I would have the inner drive. I'm glad I won't have to find out."

Ask the Experts

Still curious about how the top jockeys stack up against each other, I decided to poll a group of North America's best-known racing journalists. The questions were simple: Who are your top 10 jockeys? Who are the next 5, those you find difficult to leave out of the top 10?

To give the poll a sensible regional distribution, opinions were solicited from all along the Eastern Seaboard (where racing is concentrated in New York, New Jersey, Maryland, and Florida), the Midwestern centers of Kentucky, Chicago, and Louisiana, and the West Coast outposts of Los Angeles and San Francisco.

The 19 replies give a solid sample from across the country. The East was represented by Steven Crist (*The New York Times*), William Leggett and William Nack (*Sports Illustrtated*), Paul Moran (*Newsday*), Don Clippinger (*Philadelphia Inquirer*), Ray Kerrison (*New York Post*), Bob Harding (*Newark Star-Ledger*), Dale Austin (*Baltimore Evening Sun*), and Joe Hirsch (*Daily Racing Form*).

From the Midwest came the opinions of Maryjean Wall (*Lexington Herald-Leader*), Bob Roesler (*New Orleans Times-Picayune*), Jim Bolus (*Louisville Times*), Neil Milbert (*Chicago Sun Times*), and Dan Farley, American correspondent for England's *Racing Post* and former editor of *The Thoroughbred Record*.

The Western word came from Bill Christine (*Los Angeles Times*), Jay Privman (*Los Angeles Daily News*), Robbie Henwood (*The Blood Horse*), Mike Marten (*Daily Racing Form*, Los Angeles), and Dale Omenson (*Daily Racing Form*, San Francisco). And me, with a signed and sealed ballot placed in the hopper long before the results came rolling in.

The Verdict

Whew! Off the hook. The troops came through, validating my identification of the top jockeys. Here are the racing writers' top 10, based on number of top-10 appearances on the ballots:

Jockey	Top 10s
Pincay	20
Cordero	20
Velasquez	20
McCarron	20
Day	19
Delahoussaye	15
Stevens	11
Romero	11
Maple	10
Valenzuela	8

The results confirmed the Big Five—Pincay, Cordero, Velasquez,

McCarron, and Day. There was also broad support for Eddie Delahoussaye, the laid-back Cajun who was champion in Louisiana and Chicago before moving to California.

Interestingly, Delahoussaye lags far behind the top five when it comes to national championships. He won the most races in North America in 1978, his only title, compared to the collections of Pincay (8), McCarron (6), Cordero (4), Day (3), and Velasquez (2). Ah, but never underestimate the power of the Kentucky Derby. Delahousaaye won back-to-back Derbies in 1982 and '83, which practically guarantees him a lifelong fan club as long as he keeps his toe in the top 10.

In the second tier of the top 10, the racing writers came into conflict with our steady group of leading riders from the 1980s. They disagreed twice with the selections included in the study group, and it was obvious they were more impressed with recent achievements. The writers virtually ignored Bill Shoemaker (only 6 votes) and Richard Migliore (5), and replaced them with Gary Stevens of California and Randy Romero of New York.

Neither is a surprise. Both Stevens and Romero maintain high profiles, winning races and money in large batches wherever they go. Both are likely to be on everyone's list by the end of the decade, but neither man had the numbers to penetrate the top group based on the 1980–1985 standings.

The turf writers were in a quandary when considering the New York jockey colony and its three young lions—Romero, Migliore, and Jose Santos. Romero invaded the bigtime with an impressive portfolio, averaging 297 winners per year in the Midwest. Santos came to town in the spring of 1986 hot on the momentum of more than 400 victories over an 18-month period in Florida. Migliore, homegrown and fresh from taking the New York title in 1985, could not even sway his own constituency. His 5 votes matched Santos' total.

(As a matter of fact, only three of the nine "Eastern" writers placed Migliore among their top 10. Three listed Santos, and five picked Romero. One writer was impressed—or parochial—enough to place all three in his top 10.)

New Jersey's giant, Herb McCauley, had 4 votes, all from the Eastern bloc of writers. Fourteen more riders received either 1, 2, or 3 votes. They included Sandy Hawley, Donald MacBeth, Alex Solis, Chris Antley, Fernando Toro, Larry Snyder, Rafael Meza, Russell Baze, Jerry Bailey, Jean Cruguet, Donald Miller Jr., Ruben Hernandez, Craig Perret, and Walter Guerra.

Hard on Shoe

In the case of Shoemaker . . . well, let's face it. He was ripe for bumping. But do not think for a moment that his exclusion was a heartless, cold-blooded operation. Some of the comments (or apologies) included:

—"Feels un-American to omit, but he's not what he was."

—"I hate to leave Shoe off because to me he's like Sandy Koufax—he may not be the best of all time, but it's hard to imagine how anybody could have been better."

—"I placed him sixth, but it's a question mark if he belongs there today."

Despite Shoemaker's steady output of stakes victories and four top 10 appearances in the early '80s, he was still considered by many to be over the hill, unreliable on a day-by-day basis, interested only in big money paydays. In 1985 nonstakes races, Shoemaker won only 9.4 percent of the time, compared to a 17.7 percent winning rate in stakes races. That's great to know if you are an owner or trainer shopping for a jockey, or if you are a fan interested in betting only the top class races. Among the leading jockeys of 1985, only the upwardly mobile Gary Stevens showed a similar disparity, though on a much higher level: a 14.3 percent win rate in nonstakes and a 21.1 percent rate in stakes.

At the time the poll was taken, Shoemaker had begun thinking seriously of retirement. His mounts were down to between two and three per day. He had won only four stakes through the first four months of 1986. Then came what might have been his last hurrah, a fairytale ending to a storybook career.

Shoemaker became the oldest man—by 12 years!—to win the Kentucky Derby when he rode a long-legged chestnut named Ferdinand to victory on May 2, 1986. The sports press had a field day. Suddenly, Shoemaker was back from the grave, showing the kids how it was done. His unprecedented achievement was compared to the emotional Masters victory of 46-year-old Jack Nicklaus less than one month earlier. Nicklaus, watching the Derby at home that Saturday afternoon, is reported to have turned to his wife, Barbara, and said, "I didn't know Shoemaker was still riding."

Even though Shoemaker had been absent from the money top 10 since 1983, Ferdinand helped change all that. The Derby winner earned $981,678 in 1986 and Shoemaker finished eighth in the standings.

Purses are so huge today (the 1986 Derby was worth $609,400 compared to $228,650 in 1979) that one horse and a few races can make a jockey's year look better than it really is. Champion turf horse Cozzene earned $618,480 in 1985, which represented 19.2 percent of the year's winnings for his regular rider, Walter Guerra, while taking up only .8 percent of Guerra's time in the saddle. The mounts of Alex Solis earned $3,829,995 in 1985, 24.4 percent of which was won by just one horse, the 2-year-old Snow Chief. In 1984 Fernando Toro stayed very close to champion filly Royal Heroine. Her earnings of $1,023,500 that year made up 26 percent of Toro's total. Another dramatic example of a one-man/one-horse show took place in 1977 when Triple Crown winner and Horse of the Year Seattle Slew banked $641,370, or 23.9 percent of jockey Jean Cruguet's final figure.

Surprise Entrant

The New York-based veteran Jacinto Vasquez, 42 when the poll was taken, just missed the writers' top 10 with 7 votes, more than not only Shoemaker, but also such established young professionals as Antley, Baze, and Solis, all very much in their prime at the time. Why? Vasquez has not made a top 10 year-end list since 1977. He rides fewer than 1,000 horses per year. He even disappeared from view in 1984 when serving a one-year suspension as a result of bribery allegations (never proven in court).

Yet his solid reputation persists. One of the writers called Vasquez "the most underrated of the great riders," at first glance a baffling contradiction in terms.

However, if you mention a top horse in the past 15 years, chances are Vasquez was involved; and chances are the horse got all the headlines while the jockey went calmly about his business. Vasquez has been the regular rider of champions Ruffian, Foolish Pleasure, Revidere, Genuine Risk, Christmas Past, and What a Summer. He won the Marlboro Cup, one of New York's most prestigious races, with horses that paid $80.40, $17, and $23.80 between 1977 and 1983. He beat Secretariat twice with two different horses in 1973, the same year "Big Red" won the Triple Crown. The first two times Vasquez rode in the Kentucky Derby, he won.

Racing writers, by professional necessity, pay more attention to major races than to cheap heats featuring the sore and the slow. Since Vasquez specializes in winning stakes races—many times winning with horses given less than a decent chance—his support among racetrack journalists makes perfect sense.

In 1985, the 990 horses ridden by Vasquez brought home an average of $4,934. That figure placed him ninth on the earnings-per-mounts (EPM) list, right in the thick of it with some high-powered names. To rate high on such a list requires a maximization of every big-money opportunity. Such a statistical breakdown represents quality over quantity, the response of a rider in pressure situations. Here are the top 10 from '85:

Jockey	EPM
Pincay	$9,520
Cordero	9,114
Velasquez	8,542
McCarron	8,413
Shoemaker	6,223
Toro	5,240
Delahoussaye	5,047
Day	4,952
Vasquez	4,934
Maple	4,872

Pincay's top figure includes the $2,000,000 bonus won by Spend A Buck in the Jersey Derby. He called it the "toughest ride of my life," so give him credit. Without the bonus, Pincay's EPM figure is $8,101.

These men have reached a point in their careers when they can afford to pick and choose their rides. Most of them opt for quality over quantity, choosing to ride fewer and more select mounts than younger jockeys, who take what they can get and have the energy to ride hard seven times a day.

This is also a veteran group. Even without Shoemaker (who, at 54, was a throw-out in any age-related survey), the average age of the nine remaining jockeys was 37.2. Compare that to the average age of the top 10 race-winners of 1985—28.2—or even to the top 10 money-winners—31.8.

This list also reminds us of the reputation of Fernando Toro, whose documented abilities in turf races place him in a position to win money at a faster rate while riding fewer horses.

"I don't want to ride a lot of horses these days anyway," said the 44-year-old Toro in the spring of 1986. "Riding a lot of short races on the dirt is boring. They're all the same. I'm at a place in my career that I don't have to be bored if I don't want to. And how else can I make such a good living?"

4

What Do These People Do?: The Trainers

There is perhaps no role in sports less understood than that of the thoroughbred trainer. Ask the typical racing fan to describe the typical trainer and you come up with the following description:

Sex: Male, 99.9% of the time.
Race: Caucasian, though sometimes Latino.
Age: Anywhere from 25 to 85.
Physical attributes: Need only know how to saddle a horse.
Educational requirements: Ability to read the *Daily Racing Form*, track program and, most important of all, the odds board.
Background: Helps if you have the same last name as somebody else in the sport.
Dress code: The best of Palm Beach, Palm Springs, or Gilley's Bar.

The highest compliment a trainer can give a colleague is to call him a "good caretaker" of his horses.

When asked to define their own profession, though, American trainers usually turn to sports analogies. They call themselves a coach, general manager, talent scout, analyst, and cheerleader all rolled into one. Some use computers to keep track of training schedules, medication requirements, and eligibility. Others still mix their own secret healing potions and store them in unmarked jars.

To hold a trainer's license you must pass a state test, in most cases administered by the local stewards, a veterinarian, and other trainers. How a person gets to that point, though, is a crapshoot.

Most trainers are born to the game by way of fathers, brothers, uncles, cousins, or family friends. Others enter through side doors. Former trash collectors, CIA agents, dance teachers, salami salesmen,

professors, ski instructors, jockeys, policemen, pool sharks, car deal-
ers, and caterers have all trained thoroughbreds.

Trainers are independent operators. They charge their clients by
the horse and by the day (up to $60 per horse per day in some places),
as well as 10 percent of every winning purse. The big barns employ as
many as 35 people; the trainer becomes a ringmaster at a three-ring
circus each day. The smaller outfits get by with a groom and a hot-
walker and a trainer who gets very, very dirty.

There are no rules for learning the ropes, no college classes or
correspondence courses. You learn to become a trainer by watching
and asking questions, and then usually doing it wrong a few times on
your own.

In his 1947 book, *Training the Racehorse*, Lt. Col. Patrick Stewart,
a British horseman of impeccable repute, offered a list of maxims that
go a long way toward defining the job of trainer. Col. Stewart's advice
included:

—Study the expressions on the faces of your horses; you can then
see if they are well and happy or tired and depressed.

—Feel the temperature of the hoof with the back of your fingers—
all four of them—when you go round stables; it will show you more
than passing the hand down the leg.

—After a race, put the horse on a very light diet for two or three
days; it will help him to recover more quickly.

—Thoroughbreds vary greatly in constitution; some can come out
and win twice in one week. It is not likely to do them much good even
if they can.

—Watch the droppings of every horse in the stable. They are a
sure barometer of health or disorder.

While it's difficult to picture a trainer like the sophisticated John
Gosden sifting through a pile of manure like a seer reading tea leaves,
the point is a good one. A trainer's life is made up of quiet, incremental
decisions, which in turn lead to short-range programs for specific
horses. These programs can reveal a trainer's professional personality
and give valuable clues as to what to expect from the horses he races.
The bottom line: A horse usually determines his own fate on the track,
but it is up to the trainer to make that fate profitable.

Top Guns

Knowing the tendencies of local trainers is an absolute must if you
want to have a good day at the races. Even a cursory glance at the

"top 10" standings published in a track program can add valuable perspective to your handicapping. It is wise to pay special attention to the relatively new "winning percentage" statistic for trainers. As simple as it sounds, racetracks have only added this feature during the last few years. There is something far more reassuring about betting on a horse whose trainer wins 20 percent of the time than on one from a stable with a 10 percent success rate.

The best source of training percentages has been provided by Greg Lawlor of San Diego. Lawlor is a computer-oriented racing analyst who periodically publishes a revealing list of names and numbers— some of them damning, some highly complimentary. Before Lawlor went public with the grim details, there may have been only the dimmest perception that a particular trainer was having a bad season. Suddenly, the sports world at large had concrete evidence of ineptitude— or bad luck—when the Lawlor percentages for a certain trainer showed only two wins from 78 runners. (Lawlor breaks his studies into race classifications, as well. A trainer could have a poor record overall, yet be holding his head above water in such specific categories as maidens, turf races, or horses returning from layoffs.)

Winning percentages only scratch the surface, however. Because they have considerable latitude in placing their horses in favorable situations, trainers specializing in claiming horses may be able to record higher win percentages than those who go after allowance races or stakes. Two-year-old races are highly competitive, experimental in nature, and unpredictable. Some trainers avoid them like the plague, while others are known for their work with young horses. There are trainers who build their business around imported horses and key upon turf racing. A trainer may have unlimited resources of horseflesh or he may have to work wonders with the few animals he is given during the course of a season.

What kind of a race is a specific trainer most likely to win? Tendencies can be displayed in much the same manner that were used in analyzing jockeys in an earlier chapter. For the purposes of this study, 10 of the leading trainers of the 1980s were selected and their 1985 records examined. They come from the East, West, and Midwest. They represent everything from the high-turnover claiming game, the money in the middle of the spectrum, and the pot of gold at the end of the rainbow. Some of these trainers are predictable, others are often surprising, and it shows in the types of races they win and the prices that their horses pay.

You may not see these trainers on a regular basis. But by looking at how the best stack up in various categories, you can get an idea of how to compare the trainers at your local track. The same measurements can be taken—and hold true—wherever there is racing, whether at Belmont Park or Blue Ribbon Downs. It is the kind of information well worth considering to aid in handicapping and increase your appreciation of the sport.

All of the statistical information used to measure trainers in this chapter was culled from *Daily Racing Form* charts and the year-end statistics presented in *Daily Racing Form*'s Annual Review edition. Even the most remote racetracks, as long as they are validated by a state racing commission, are monitored by the *Daily Racing Form.* Beyond that, each local racetrack usually has a statistician on staff who is available to the public. Local newspapers publish the results of races, and track programs provide detailed information on race descriptions and trainer standings. There are really no secrets to the numbers of racing. *Interpretation* is the key.

Our Ten

Here are our 10 top trainers, ready to bare their 1985 statistics to the world. After we're through, they'll know how the frog felt in high school biology. (Remember, though, these principles of dissection apply to thoroughbred trainers anywhere, anytime.) The 10 are:

—King T. Leatherbury, the self-styled "king" of the claimers. You can find his horses in action nearly every day on the Maryland circuit. They are the walking wounded, the magnificent cripples, running on heart and borrowed time. Leatherbury has turned the short-term profit of claimers into an art form.

—Woody Stephens, the dean of the New York colony, and Charlie Whittingham, his California counterpart, between them winners of more major races than the next 10 men on the list. (Once they collaborated briefly in the training of a 2-year-old named Stephan's Odyssey. The result was predictable—Stephan's Odyssey won the $1,140,000 Hollywood Futurity. The only real shock was the winning payoff—an outrageous $24.40.)

—Claude R. McGaughey III, nicknamed "Shug" (as in "sugar"). What a sweet career he will have before it's over. A disciple of David Whiteley (more on him later), from the Stephens-Whittingham school of quality over quantity. McGaughey hit the top 10 for the first time in 1985. He prides himself on a high percentage of winners.

—Bobby Frankel, the epitome of the "Yeah, what's it to ya?" New Yorker. Frankel began life as a claiming trainer in the East and then miraculously metamorphosed into a manager of classy European imports and well-bred youngsters in the West. "They eat the same amount as cheap horses and they make more money," Frankel insists. "What's to choose?"

—Jack Van Berg and his most successful disciple, William Mott. Van Berg has won more races than any thoroughbred trainer in history, while operating a string of stables from coast to coast. Mott concentrated his early career on the Midwest and so far is following in Van Berg's footsteps as a winner.

—John Gosden and Lazaro Barrera, for a bit of foreign flavor. Barrera, the man from Havana, has two Kentucky Derby winners to his credit, is already in the Hall of Fame, and shows no signs of slowing down. Gosden, a Cambridge grad, is half Charlie Whittingham's age and seems intent upon catching the old master.

—And D. (for Darrell) Wayne Lukas, the man who has redefined training in his own corporate image.

Running Numbers

As we chop up the 1985 records of our 10 study trainers, some of the pieces will resemble those studied in the jockey chapter, which makes sense, since the role of the rider is essentially an extension of the efforts of the trainer. (There isn't a trainer alive who would not prefer to dispense with the racing and award prize money to those horses judged "best trained." Of course, we know who the judges would be.)

These are the training categories we'll look at:

Maidens. Winning with unproven horses.
Claimers. Winning with cheap and sore horses.
Quality. Winning the best races.
Ages. Trends with 2-year-olds, 3-year-olds, and 4-year-olds and up.
Fillies. A different game?
Turf runners. A taste of the old country.
Prices. Trainers it may pay to play.

Efficiency. Who goes through the most horses? Who makes winners of the most horses? Whose horses win more often?

The Assembly Line

It makes a big difference, especially to a prospective owner, to find out which trainer can give him the most for his money. Trainers can wave impressive gross figures all they want. What it comes down to—what it *should* come down to—is efficiency. In other words, getting the most out of the animals. There are ways to measure success in this area—let's look at some 1985 figures first:

Trainer	Starts	Wins	Horses	Winners
Barrera	475	64	78	41
Frankel	375	74	84	42
Gosden	451	77	113	45
Leatherbury	870	186	172	104
Lukas	1,140	218	187	92
McGaughey	395	94	87	49
Mott	695	153	127	69
Stephens	262	53	50	29
Van Berg	1,663	234	312	158
Whittingham	464	68	96	36

The baseline figure for a trainer's ongoing performance has always been the number of starts made by his horses and the total wins accumulated. This table goes on to add the number of horses it took to make those starts, and, in a further refinement, exactly how many of those horses were actually winners at some point in the season. The results lead to the following breakdown:

Trainer	Win%	WPH	SPH	%Wnrs	WPW
Barrera	13.3%	0.81	6.09	52.5%	1.53
Frankel	19.7%	0.88	4.46	50.0%	1.76
Gosden	17.0%	0.68	3.99	39.8%	1.71
Leatherbury	21.4%	1.08	5.05	60.4%	1.79
Lukas	14.0%	0.75	5.33	49.2%	2.37
McGaughey	23.8%	1.08	4.54	56.3%	1.92
Mott	22.0%	1.20	5.47	54.3%	2.22
Stephens	20.2%	1.06	5.24	58.0%	1.82
Van Berg	14.0%	0.75	5.33	50.6%	1.48
Whittingham	14.7%	0.71	4.83	37.5%	1.89

Call this an "activity" table. On the surface, each trainer wins a certain percentage of his starts. Beyond that, we now know the average number of starts he gets per horse (SPH), the average number of wins per horse (WPH), the percent of horses under his care that actually become winners (%Wnrs), and the average number of wins to be expected from each of those winners (WPW). Now, on to the money.

Trainer	Earnings	EPS	EPH
Barrera	$ 2,668,339	$ 5,618	$34,209
Frankel	3,571,703	9,525	42,520
Gosden	3,263,176	7,235	28,878
Leatherbury	1,504,757	1,730	8,749
Lukas	11,155,188	9,654	59,653
McGaughey	3,179,697	8,050	36,548
Mott	3,469,196	4,992	27,317
Stephens	3,323,009	12,683	66,460
Van Berg	4,626,821	2,782	14,830
Whittingham	5,895,873	12,707	61,415

Earnings per start (EPS) is a good way for the trainer to keep score; but since most trainers are employed by several owners, the earnings per horse (EPH) column tells a more revealing story in terms of individual expectations.

Are We Any Smarter?

Absolutely. We now know that a horse trained by King Leatherbury had an excellent chance of winning at least one race during the year (60.4 percent of them did), but also of not winning much money ($8,749 per horse for the year).

This gives us some insight into the economic aspects of owning a racehorse. An owner who competes for less money should pay less for the upkeep of his horses. Right? Wrong. Not if that owner races in Maryland (or any state with a similar purse structure). On the Leatherbury circuit, available purses averaged $94,632 per day in 1985. The cost of racing a thoroughbred for a year in Maryland is about $15,000. Compare those figures to New York or Southern California, where average daily purses surpass $200,000 and the average horse costs $20,000 to maintain for a year. In California a horse can run for more than twice the money while incurring only about 33 percent more in training costs.

The table illustrates how vastly different training operations can be considered equally successful depending on how the figures are interpreted. The numbers tell us that Woody Stephens ranks just behind Leatherbury in producing winners (58.0 percent to 60.4 percent). Stephens, however, develops his horses from scratch, while Leatherbury claims known commodities and squeezes out a few more wins. Stephens-trained horses, however, take a lot more home to mama—an average of $66,460 per horse during the 1985 season, tops on our select list.

Common sense tells us that claiming horses earn far less money than stakes horses, and that New York horses have a shot at more money than Maryland-based thoroughbreds. Exactly how much more is a surprise. Top class horses, such as those trained by Stephens, can earn five, six, or even seven times more money. The Stephens EPH figure even exceeds that of Wayne Lukas. Despite amassing more than $11,000,000 in purses, the 187 Lukas horses earned an average of $59,653, third behind both Stephens and Whittingham in that particular column.

Now let's take a look at our top 10 trainers, comparing their winning percentages in each of 10 categories. This kind of study can be extremely useful in handicapping local races. Some trainers can be completely ignored when they start a particular type of horse; others must be consistently feared when they play to a "strength." A fan could become an expert on claiming races, or 2-year-old races, or turf races by simply knowing which trainers win those races most often.

Claiming Races

King Leatherbury wins this division, but only because he is obsessed. He goes head-to-head against a hard-nosed league of claiming trainers throughout the Maryland season. They shuffle horses around, drop them down the price ladder, and keep their owners in constant action (or agitation, depending on their success). Leatherbury's dominance of the Maryland claiming game is so thorough that he has developed a national reputation. But in so doing he neglects many of the other categories—69.3 percent of his total starters in 1985 came in claiming races. Among the other trainers who played the claiming game with any regularity, only William Mott approaches Leatherbury's winning percentage. Of Mott's starters, 32.2 percent were in claimers, indicating a more balanced approach to the business.

CLAIMING

Trainer	Starters	Wins	Win%
Barrera	58	6	10.3
Frankel	70	15	21.4
Gosden	59	8	13.5
Leatherbury	603	149	24.7
Lukas	151	25	16.5
McGaughey	26	7	26.9
Mott	208	50	24.0
Stephens	0	0	0.0
Van Berg	688	113	16.4
Whittingham	41	1	2.4

Does Woody Stephens know what a claiming race is? Why did Charlie Whittingham even bother? If McGaughey had so much success with so few claimers, why didn't he try more? Questions like these will come to mind when local trainers are studied. The profit will be in the answers.

Quality C

Quality C races are the next step up on the class ladder. It's the category with the most variety, and usually provides the most opportunities. At the minor league level, these can be the best races around. In the majors, a race worth $39,999 or less can be a steppingstone for a stakes horse on the rise, or a last chance for a horse on the way down to the claiming division.

QUALITY C

Trainer	Starters	Wins	Win%
Barrera	146	16	11.0
Frankel	133	27	20.3
Gosden	137	28	20.4
Leatherbury	96	13	13.5
Lukas	402	73	18.1
McGaughey	165	39	23.6
Mott	282	66	23.4
Stephens	116	19	16.4
Van Berg	380	51	13.4
Whittingham	104	19	18.3

Leatherbury's relatively weak percentage here may show why he deals primarily with claimers. Barrera's figure shows just how bad a year 1985 was for him. Ordinarily, the California and New York fans could rely upon Barrera to win these races at about the same rate as Frankel, Gosden, or Whittingham. Mott and McGaughey, who competed directly at several Midwestern tracks in 1985, fought to a virtual tie in terms of their Quality C winning percentages.

Quality A & B Races

Bobby Frankel decided he was tired of draining fluid from knees and ankles, tired of masking the pain of sore old horses, tired of being a claiming trainer. In essence, he changed careers in midlife.

You've got to hand it to Frankel. He has made the transition with flying colors. As recently as 1981, stakes horses contributed only 19 percent to the total earnings of his stable. By 1984, more than half the bankroll was supplied by top class horses. Today, the percentage is even higher.

Frankel still wins the occasional claiming race (one out of every five wins in 1985), but he continues to phase out the old Bobby. In doing so he has entered the lion's den occupied by the big money specialists like Whittingham, Lukas, Stephens, and Gosden. The following table shows how our 10 trainers fared in 1985 when it came to winning races worth $40,000 to $99,999 (Quality B) and races worth $100,000 or more (Quality A):

QUALITY A

Trainer	Starters	Wins	Win%
Barrera	38	5	13.2
Frankel	52	8	15.4
Gosden	49	7	14.3
Leatherbury	9	0	0.0
Lukas	118	25	21.1
McGaughey	40	5	12.5
Mott	42	11	26.2
Stephens	41	9	21.9
Van Berg	60	3	5.0
Whittingham	98	19	19.4

QUALITY B

Trainer	Starters	Wins	Win%
Barrera	81	16	19.8
Frankel	53	10	18.9
Gosden	101	17	16.8

Trainer	Starters	Wins	Win%
Leatherbury	9	1	1.1
Lukas	185	45	24.3
McGaughey	35	9	25.7
Mott	46	8	17.4
Stephens	25	6	24.0
Van Berg	93	9	9.7
Whittingham	113	16	14.2

Whittingham and Stephens are the classic big money trainers. Even though there are fewer A races than B races out there to win, these guys still win more A races than B races. The sheer number of Lukas starters in these races is impressive, but even more incredible is the rate at which his stable wins. On the downside, Leatherbury can hardly be faulted for low percentages in this area because he has practically nothing to run in A and B races. But what is Van Berg's excuse? Sure, 41 percent of his starters in 1985 were in claiming races; but the 9.2 percent that started in Quality A and B races won only 5.1 percent of the stable total. They may have won proportionately more purse money, but that doesn't help the guy in the stands at all.

Local trainers also develop reputations as "class" trainers or "claiming" trainers. Before falling for the party line, take the time to examine a reputation against reality with some counting, adding, and analysis of your own.

Turf Racing

John Gosden, hailed by many as the next Charlie Whittingham, is more than halfway toward catching his mentor. Gosden never really trained at the foot of the master, but the young Englishman has watched Whittingham like a hawk. In the following table on turf racing, take special note of the Whittingham and Gosden figures:

TURF			
Trainer	Starters	Wins	Win%
Barrera	135	19	14.1
Frankel	134	23	16.0
Gosden	242	50	20.7
Leatherbury	21	4	19.0
Lukas	124	10	8.1
McGaughey	34	4	11.7
Mott	71	14	19.7
Stephens	67	11	16.4

Trainer	Starters	Wins	Win%
Van Berg	167	14	8.4
Whittingham	240	34	14.2

Apparently, the student can teach the teacher a few things. Not only was Gosden's win percentage in turf races more than 6 points higher than Whittingham's, but it also was the best of the entire group. Of course, we must throw out Leatherbury (they don't offer many turf races for claimers) and McGaughey (can't win if you don't try). The rest of the group, however, had decent representation in turf competition.

Gosden's clientele is almost entirely European. Most of his horses begin their careers in England, Ireland, or France and then—if they are not of championship caliber—are shipped to California to continue their careers in a totally different context.

Gosden does his best to provide a smooth transition for such world travelers. His imports get time off after they arrive, and then are brought along slowly until they have fully acclimated to American food, American racing surfaces, and American training techniques. Obviously, Gosden's program has succeeded.

Whittingham has his share of European clients, as well. But while Gosden usually gets horses of midrange ability (the rough equivalent of Quality B foreigners), Whittingham is sent the cream—horses just below championship quality.

That is why Gosden wins claiming races and Whittingham avoids them like fleas: Some of Gosden's imports are untested and end up in claiming events; Whittingham, on the other hand, knows exactly what he is getting, and they ain't claimers.

4-Year-Olds and Up

Apparently, William Mott got his fill of cheap horses during his years as one of Jack Van Berg's many assistants. In 1985, his first big year on his own, Mott exhibited a tendency to win the best possible races in his neighborhood, which was primarily the Midwestern outposts of Churchill Downs, Arlington Park, Keeneland, and Oaklawn Park.

The weaning process is slow, however, and Mott still had a link with the Van Berg philosophy in one respect—the dominance of older horses in his stable. Mott's record with 4-year-olds and up—the hardened pros of the game—was better than any other trainer in the group.

That in itself is impressive, because there are more races for older horses, more money to be won, and more betting opportunities for the fans:

4 AND OLDER

Trainer	Starters	Wins	Win%
Barrera	263	37	14.0
Frankel	221	46	20.8
Gosden	289	51	17.6
Leatherbury	412	99	24.0
Lukas	451	91	24.0
McGaughey	97	23	23.7
Mott	389	100	25.7
Stephens	17	5	29.4
Van Berg	876	124	14.2
Whittingham	309	47	15.2

3-Year-Olds

Then there's Woody, who never met a 4-year-old he liked. That is a bit of an exaggeration, but the figures prove the point.

The Stephens stable is monolithic, variations on the same theme. The Stephens horse is a well-bred, precocious, stakes-caliber 2-year-old or 3-year-old with a glowing reputation even before it runs its first race. Few of the Stephens horses are kept a secret, either, as we will see later in the payoff table.

A group high 68.3 percent of Stephens' starters were 3-year-olds in 1985. Here is how he—and the others—did with the division:

3-YEAR-OLDS

Trainer	Starters	Wins	Win%
Barrera	155	15	9.6
Frankel	116	24	19.0
Gosden	159	25	15.7
Leatherbury	379	77	20.3
Lukas	433	79	18.2
McGaughey	222	51	22.9
Mott	237	37	15.6
Stephens	179	35	19.6
Van Berg	649	91	14.0
Whittingham	127	17	13.4

Stephens was 72 when he won the Belmont Stakes (for 3-year-olds) for the fifth consecutive time in 1986. Immediately, talk resumed of his pending retirement. It's been "pending" for the last decade. The Stephens story is a self-fulfilling prophecy. "I can't retire," he says. "I've got 20 beautiful babies on the farms that'll be two next year, and there just might be a Swale or a Conquistador Cielo among 'em." As long as he is Woody Stephens, he will always have that excuse.

2-Year-Olds

Stephens appears to have an heir to the throne in "Shug" Mc-Gaughey, whose 3-year-old starters made up 56 percent of his overall total in 1985. McGaughey was even more dominant than Stephens when it came to the "baby" division, or the 2-year-olds.

2-YEAR-OLDS

Trainers	Starters	Wins	Win%
Barrera	57	11	19.3
Frankel	28	4	14.3
Gosden	3	1	33.3
Leatherbury	79	10	12.6
Lukas	256	48	18.7
McGaughey	76	21	27.6
Mott	69	17	24.6
Stephens	66	13	19.7
Van Berg	138	20	14.5
Whittingham	28	3	14.3

Gosden obviously believes that a 2-year-old is a creature that should not be asked for more than eating, sleeping, and light exercise. Whittingham and Frankel are not far behind in that philosophy. Yet there are great sums of money to be made by racing a 2-year-old, and potentially great sums made by betting on them as well. The key is knowing which trainers are serious about winning early and often with young horses and which trainers are simply going through the motions to give a young horse experience. As a handicapper, I appreciate a trainer who might start an inexperienced horse every few weeks a lot more than a trainer who starts them all the time . . . and rarely wins.

Maidens

By logical extension, McGaughey was also the star of the maiden ranks. It stands to reason that a trainer who has success with 2-year-olds (mostly in maiden races) also will succeed more often with 3-year-olds starting for the first time, or trying to win for the first time.

MAIDENS

Trainers	Starters	Wins	Win%
Barrera	153	20	13.1
Frankel	67	14	20.8
Gosden	105	17	16.2
Leatherbury	153	23	15.0
Lukas	284	50	
McGaughey	129	34	26.3
Mott	117	19	16.2
Stephens	80	19	23.8
Van Berg	442	59	13.3
Whittingham	108	13	12.0

Ladies' Man—Fillies

When Wayne Lukas goes shopping for a racehorse, he usually buys a filly. For reliable investment purposes, a filly beats a colt almost every time. Even a filly with a so-so record at the races can have substantial value as a broodmare, as long as she has marketable bloodlines and a healthy constitution. On the other hand, a colt, once retired, must sell himself many times over to justify his dozens of stud fees.

Between 1982 and 1986, Lukas trained five different female champions—Landaluce, Althea, Life's Magic, Family Style, and Lady's Secret. It is hardly a surprise that he had more than 100 filly winners in 1985, along with one of the best winning percentages among our 10 trainers.

FILLIES

Trainer	Starters	Wins	Win%
Barrera	144	17	11.8
Frankel	104	17	16.3
Gosden	192	27	14.1
Leatherbury	316	54	17.1
Lukas	546	101	18.5
McGaughey	223	38	17.0
Mott	296	68	22.9
Stephens	98	23	23.5
Van Berg	609	87	14.3
Whittingham	142	22	15.5

Mott also displayed an uncanny ability to handle fillies, and because of that he came to the attention of some high-powered breeders. He eventually accepted the job as private trainer for Bert Firestone, who has owned such champions as Genuine Risk, Honest Pleasure, and April Run.

Happy Returns

This is the table that we can all relate to—mutuel payoffs.

The arbitrary demarcation line will be $10 win payoffs. The purpose is to illustrate the tendencies of our 10 trainers to win at odds of 4–1 and up, or of less than 4–1. The percentages represent the percentage of winners at each range of odds, not of overall starters, answering the question, "When this trainer wins, what is the horse likely to pay?"

PAYOFFS

Trainer	$10 and Up%	Less than $10%
Barrera	30.6	69.4
Frankel	28.4	71.6
Gosden	36.4	63.6
Leatherbury	23.7	76.3
Lukas	25.7	74.3
McGaughey	21.3	78.7
Mott	23.4	76.6
Stephens	9.4	90.6
Van Berg	32.3	67.7
Whittingham	22.1	77.9

Gosden boasts the leading figure among the $10-plus payoffs on winners. The reason is apparent. Handicappers have been slow to educate themselves on foreign racing. The European past performance lines in the *Daily Racing Form* just barely resemble North American lines. There are no internal fractions, no speed ratings, no track variants, no points of call. European races are usually metric in length, though sometimes measured in vague "about" distances. Final times for the same apparent distances vary wildly. Gosden's Europeans pose a handicapping puzzle that has yet to be solved, in spite of the valiant efforts of men like James Quinn, who publishes a handbook of major European races each year for the edification of the baffled American fan.

Who's Our "Most Valuable Trainer"?

It all depends upon the measuring stick, just as it will when you evaluate trainers at your hometown racetrack. Want to bet on a turf race? Wait for a Gosden runner to show up, and keep your distance from a Lukas horse. Looking at maidens, especially 2-year-olds? McGaughey is your man. Fillies? In this bunch, Woody Stephens is the name to look for. Leatherbury is the reigning king of the claiming game, but the old boss, Bobby Frankel, still keeps his hand in with a fine percentage.

The trainer who scored highest across the board, however, was William Mott. With his fingers in every pie—maidens, claimers, turf races, and quality events—he maintained a consistently high percentage in nearly every column:

MOTT'S SCORECARD

Fillies	2nd	Claimers	3rd
Turf	2nd	Maidens	5th (tie)
2-Year-Olds	2nd	Quality B	5th
3-Year-Olds	7th	Quality C	2nd
4 and Older	1st	Quality A	1st

Mott is truly an exception to the rule. Not all trainers can succeed so often in so many different ways. Not many of them even try. Just remember: Such an analysis of trainer tendencies—and consistencies—is worthwhile only if it can be applied in all cases and at all racetracks. It can. And it can make you a better handicapper and a more knowledgeable fan.

Raising the Stakes

Until 1920, the most home runs hit in a single season was 29. Then, in 1920, Babe Ruth broke his own record by hitting 54.

Wayne Lukas is the Babe Ruth of trainers, at least when it comes to breaking his own records. In 1984 the man from Wisconsin trashed Jack Van Berg's single season earnings mark of $4,587,457 by posting a $5,835,921. "We can do better," Lukas promised.

One year later, the Lukas organization, a nationwide network of strategically located stables, had nearly doubled its record output of 1984. The Lukas 1985 total was $11,155,188, nearly twice that of second-place Charlie Whittingham, whose $5,895,873 was also good enough to break the old mark.

Lukas and Van Berg have similar operations. Both of them make their headquarters in California while directing "branch offices" in the East and Midwest. Both of them spend more time on the phone than the average teenager, and both have trained assistants to follow in their own image and philosophy.

Lukas, however, has specialized in a higher grade of racehorse. One look at the quality race tables on page 183 and it is easy to see the difference. Van Berg's horses won three races worth more than $100,000 in 1985, representing just 1.3 percent of the stable's winning activity. Lukas runners won 25 "hundred-granders" in 1985, 11.4 percent of the stable wins. (Only Whittingham could boast a more impressive figure in Quality A races. For Charlie, there are no races under $100,000 worth winning. His stable's 19 Quality A wins represent 27.9 percent of his total.

Don't be misled, however. Lukas wins his share of cheap races. He sent his claimers to Ak-Sar-Ben racetrack in Nebraska and won them in bunches. His great strength is management. He looks at a horse with the cold, heartless eye of an accountant and decides when and where that horse can win, whether it is at Aqueduct in the winter, Saratoga in the summer, or Bay Meadows in the fall. More often than not, he is right.

Lukas takes pride in his uncanny ability to wade through a herd of yearlings and purchase the "true athlete" in the crowd. In 1977 he bought one yearling at auction, a daughter of Secretariat, spending $500,000 of his own money and then selling it to a client. The filly, Terlingua, turned out to be the fastest female of her generation, ended up winning $423,896, and was worth five times her purchase price as a broodmare.

But even Wayne Lukas can be fooled. The yearling market may be the world's biggest roulette wheel. In 1982 and '83 Lukas maintained a high profile at the most prestigious sales and came away with several big numbers. These young horses showed him just as much promise as did Terlingua. Somewhere along the way, however, the dream fizzled:

Horse	Sire	Price	Earnings to 7–86
Louisiana Slew	Seattle Slew	$2,900,000	$ 75,298
Santiago Peak	Alydar	1,600,000	16,118
Devils River	Seattle Slew	1,000,000	0

Horse	Sire	Price	Earnings to 7–86
Bonanno	Raja Baba	500,000	no starts
Claude France	Raja Baba	500,000	25,780
Huddle Up	Sir Ivor	425,000	63,542
Butterfield Stage	Nijinsky II	410,000	3,960
Commissioner Pete	Alydar	400,000	no starts
Blue Sheep	Raja Baba	400,000	16,864
Mighty Lady	Raja Baba	350,000	4,800
Ahree Covair	Exclusive Native	270,000	19,485
Fiesty Fouts	Northern Jove	230,000	25,025
Totals		$9,665,000	$250,872

Hitting the Jackpot

Not even a man like Lukas, with his overpowering personality, could survive in business with such a record. There is, of course, another side of the ledger, representing high-priced yearlings who paid off or bargain basement buys that turned into gold mines. Again, keying upon the Lukas yearling purchases of 1982 and '83, here are the happy endings:

Horse	Sire	Price	Earnings to 7–86
Saratoga Six	Alydar	$2,200,000	$ 304,940
Pancho Villa	Secretariat	1,800,000	584,734
Life at the Top	Seattle Slew	800,000	408,102
Tank's Prospect	Mr. Prospector	625,000	1,355,845
Fiesta Lady	Secretariat	525,000	177,160
Clear Choice	Raise a Native	475,000	199,476
Twilight Ridge	Cox's Ridge	350,000	705,888
Nervous Baba	Raja Baba	235,000	119,468
Family Style	State Dinner	60,000	1,130,248
Sovereign Don	Sovereign Dancer	40,000	215,858
Totals		$7,110,000	$5,201,519

Add the following residual benefits from horses on the this list:
—Saratoga Six, injured and retired after four races, was syndicated for $350,000 a share based on 40 shares.
—As a broodmare, Fiesta Lady was sold for $2,200,000 (in foal to Alydar) in the fall of 1985. A similar happy fate awaited Family Style, Twilight Ridge, and Nervous Baba.
—Midway through 1986 it appeared as if Life at the Top (winner of the Mother Goose Stakes), Clear Choice (winner of the Withers

Stakes and Swaps Stakes), and Family Style had good paydays still to come.

Where It Happened

Describing the Lukas stable as national is almost an understatement. If it were cost-feasible, the man would be running horses in Bangkok. Basically, the large Lukas stables were in action at eight tracks in 1985, listed below with the winning percentage at each course:

Ak-Sar-Ben	23.4%	**Del Mar**	16.3%
Aqueduct	25.5%	**Hollywood Park**	5.5%
Bay Meadows	15.7%	**Santa Anita**	10.6%
Belmont Park	32.5%	**Saratoga**	30.0%

There was also a highly successful mini-invasion to Oaklawn Park in Arkansas, where Lukas won with four of the seven horses he sent out, and isolated victories at Pimlico, Monmouth Park, Golden Gate Fields, Philadelphia Park, Hawthorne, and the Meadowlands. Believe it or not, the proud members of the Lukas cavalry were not invincible. They failed in various forays to Turf Paradise, Latonia, Keeneland, Churchill Downs, Laurel, Garden State Park, Gulfstream Park, Keystone, Suffolk Downs, and the Pomona Fairgrounds near Los Angeles.

Stakes Were Far from Rare

In 1985 there were 2,633 stakes races run in North America won by 1,734 horses out of 82,471 total runners. Of the 3,253 active trainers listed in the American Racing Manual, one man, Wayne Lukas, won 70 of those stakes. Lukas needed only 25 different horses to win those 70 stakes, giving us a numerical coincidence that reads:

—Using .03 percent of the overall racehorse population, one man, representing a similar .03 percent of the trainer population, won 2.63 percent of the stakes races offered in North America in 1985.

Lukas stakes horses collected their prizes at 15 different racetracks in eight different states. Of the 70 stakes wins, 38 (54.2 percent) were graded races, regarded the toughest to win. It was an amazing accomplishment. Literally, one out of every three Lukas winners in 1985 came in a stakes event.

The only short-term threat to the Lukas mark would come from Lukas himself; in 1986 that is exactly what happened. Midway through

November he broke his 1985 record, well on his way to a $12,000,000 year and another stakes-winning mark in the bargain. In the face of such dominance, the first year of a historical trend is usually the most interesting. Here, for posterity, is his 1985 miracle year in retrospect:

Date	Track	Horse	Race-Grade	Payoff
1-5	BM	Lady's Secret	Hail Hilarious S.	$ 3.40
1-6	BM	Rain on My Parade	Spectacular S.	7.40
1-9	SA	Wising Up	Pasadena S.	6.00
1-26	AQU	Imp Society	Assault H.-III	5.20
1-30	SA	Wising Up	Santa Ynez S.-III	5.80
2-3	BM	Tank's Prospect	El Camino Derby-III	6.80
2-16	AQU	Imp Society	Stymie H.-III	3.20
3-3	AQU	Imp Society	Grey Lag H.-III	5.00
3-16	PIM	Imp Society	J.B. Campbell H.-III	3.20
3-17	SA	Image of Greatness	San Felipe H.-I	8.60
3-23	AQU	Pancho Villa	Bay Shore S.-II	30.80
4-6	AQU	Gene's Lady	Fair Mist H.	5.60
4-6	OP	Imp Society	Razorback H.-II	3.00
4-16	OP	Lady's Secret	Prima Donna H.	3.60
4-19	OP	Imp Society	Oaklawn H.-II	3.60
4-20	OP	Tank's Prospect	Arkansas Derby-I	8.20
5-4	AQU	Mt. Livermore	Carter H.-II	27.60
5-18	PIM	Tank's Prospect	Preakness S.-I	11.40
5-18	AQU	Life's Magic	Shuvee H.-II	8.20
5-25	AKS	Something Gorgeous	His Majesty's Cncl.S.	7.60
5-26	BEL	Lady's Secret	Bowl of Flowers S.	3.00
6-8	AKS	Something Gorgeous	4h S.	3.60
6-8	BEL	Alabama Nana	Genuine Risk S.	4.20
6-8	BEL	Mt. Livermore	Jaipur S.	4.20
6-12	GG	Arewehavingfunyet	Time to Leave S.	6.60
6-18	MTH	Wising Up	Revidere S.	4.80
6-22	MTH	Lady's Secret	Regret H.	2.80
6-22	AKS	Ritzy Lady	River City Roundup H.	3.40
6-28	HOL	Le Slew	B. Thoughtful S.	8.40
6-29	HOL	Pancho Villa	Silver Screen H.-II	9.00
6-30	BEL	Twilight Ridge	Astoria S.-III	2.80
7-6	AKS	Imp Society	Board of Govs. H.	2.60
7-6	HOL	Arewehavingfunyet	Landaluce S.-III	7.80
7-6	BEL	Lady's Secret	Rose S.	2.80
7-14	BEL	Sovereign Don	Tremont S.-III	7.60
8-1	SAR	Lady's Secret	Test S.-II	22.20
8-2	SAR	Sovereign Don	Saratoga Special-II	10.20
8-9	SAR	Lady's Secret	Ballerina S.-II	3.80
8-10	AKS	Something Social	My Juliet S.	15.60
8-10	SAR	Let It Fly	Countess Jane S.	7.00
8-14	SAR	Sovereign Don	Sanford S.-II	13.20
8-15	SAR	Nervous Baba	Adirondack S.-II	7.60
8-17	SAR	Pancho Villa	King's Bishop H.	7.20

Date	Track	Horse	Race-Grade	Payoff
8-19	DMR	Arewehavingfunyet	Sorrento S.	5.80
8-23	AKS	Special Kinda Guy	Vale of Tears S.	6.20
8-26	SAR	Family Style	Spinaway S.-I	6.60
9-1	DMR	Arewehavingfunyet	Del Mar Debutante-II	3.40
9-7	HAW	Family Style	Lassie S.-I	3.40
9-7	BEL	Lady's Secret	Maskette S.-I	4.00
9-8	BEL	Mt. Livermore	Boojum H.-III	15.40
9-14	PHA	Le Slew	Doylestown H.	5.20
9-22	BEL	Lady's Secret	Ruffian H.-I	2.60
9-27	BM	Special Kinda Guy	San Joaquin Inv.	19.00
9-28	BEL	Alabama Nana	Leixable S.	7.40
9-28	BEL	Ketoh	Cowdin S.-I	3.20
10-2	SA	Louisiana Slew	Sunny Slope S.	6.60
10-5	BEL	Mt. Livermore	Fall Highweight H.-II	6.00
10-12	SA	Arewehavingfunyet	Oak Leaf S.-I	3.40
10-13	BEL	Lady's Secret	Beldame S.-I	3.20
10-14	BEL	Family Style	Frizette S.-I	4.40
10-23	AQU	Alabama Nana	First Flight H.-III	2.80
11-2	AQU	Twilight Ridge	BC Juvenile Fillies-I	3.20
11-2	AQU	Life's Magic	BC Distaff-I	2.80
11-15	MED	Gene's Lady	Dottie's Doll S.	3.40
11-23	BM	North Sider	San Jose H.	5.00
11-30	HOL	Pancho Villa	National Sprint-III	15.20
12-14	PHA	Gene's Lady	Whitemarsh H.	4.80
12-15	BM	North Sider	Foster City S.	2.80
12-22	AQU	Taj Alriyadh	Roamer H.	3.40
12-28	BM	North Sider	Bay Meadows Debutante	2.80

Abbreviations key: AKS—Ak-Sar-Ben, Omaha; AQU—Aqueduct, New York; BM—Bay Meadows, San Francisco; BEL—Belmont Park, New York; DMR—Del Mar, California; GG—Golden Gate Fields, San Francisco; HAW—Hawthorne Racecourse, Chicago; HOL—Hollywood Park, Los Angeles; MED—Meadowlands, New Jersey; MTH—Monmouth Park, New Jersey; PHA—Philadelphia Park, Pennsylvania; OP—Oaklawn Park, Hot Springs, Arkansas; PIM—Pimlico, Baltimore; SA—Santa Anita Park, Los Angeles; SAR—Saratoga, New York S = Stakes, H = Handicap

A $2.00 win bet on each of the 278 Lukas stakes entries would have resulted in a net loss of $79.40. A wise gambler would have keyed instead on the Lukas stakes horses in New York, where the stable racked up 33 of the 70 wins, some of them at outrageous prices.

Pancho Villa's $30.80 upset of the March 23 Bay Shore Stakes at Aqueduct was more the rule than the exception. Mt. Livermore clicked at $27.60 in the May 4 Carter Handicap; Life's Magic paid a generous $8.20 in the May 18 Shuvee Handicap; and Lady's Secret, a popular gamble all summer long, was abandoned by the Saratoga fans when she faced Mom's Command in the August 1 Test Stakes. The unfaithful were burned, as Lady's Secret won and returned $22.20. The upstate

New Yorkers never did believe in Sovereign Don. He paid $10.20 and $13.20 in his two stakes victories at Saratoga. And Mt. Livermore had one more surprise in the September 8 Boojum Handicap back at Belmont when he paid off at $15.40.

More for Less

He was blessed. When he walked through the racetrack the hardcore gamblers swore he gave off that weird glow of invincibility. He could have started a church and the flocks would have gathered. It was among the greatest seasons recorded by any trainer in the modern history of racing, and today hardly anyone remembers it.

David Anders Whiteley, bespectacled, chain-smoking, second-generation horseman, won with practically everything he touched during an unforgettable 1979 campaign. The raw numbers reveal a stable that earned $1,695,515, good for eighth place behind Lazaro Barrera's league-leading $3,608,517. Certainly nothing in the neighborhood of the Lukasian $11 million. But take a look at how Whiteley's horses earned that $1.6 million.

The stable sent out only 91 starters the entire year. They won 34 races (37.3 percent), finished second 16 times and third 13 times for a 1-2-3 rate of 69.2 percent. The next lowest number of starters on the top 10 list was the 315 saddled by Woody Stephens. Simple math tell us that everytime a Whiteley horse ran it brought home an average check of $18,632. Compare that to Barrera's $7,334 or Woody's $6,385 or even Charlie Whittingham's $5,597 that same season. Nobody, not even the D. Wayne Lukas juggernaut of 1985 with its $9,785 per start has ever equaled such extraordinary efficiency at such a high level.

The only comparable achievement to Whiteley's 1979 total occurred in 1984 when Stephens amassed $5,223,163 at a rate of $18,788 per start. Another remarkable performance, true, but one that must be considered second to Whiteley's if inflation is taken into account. The Consumer Price Index had risen by 43.1 percent between 1979 and 1984, and any comparison of purses must be viewed in this statistical light. In terms of "constant dollars," Whiteley's 1979 figure becomes $26,662 when translated to the racing world of 1984.

Based on at least 75 starters, here are some of the other top earnings-per-start trainers in North America since Whiteley's unprecedented 1979:

Year	Trainer	Purse Total	Starts	EPS
1980	Angel Penna	$1,468,282	145	$10,126
1981	C. Whittingham	3,993,302	376	10,620
1982	C. Whittingham	4,587,457	410	11,189
1983	Woody Stephens	3,342,303	286	11,686
1984	Mack Miller	1,807,317	147	12,294
1985	Woody Stephens	3,323,009	262	12,683
1985	Neil Drysdale	2,743,416	248	11,062

Why is this significant? Racing at its highest levels has few replacement parts. Claimers and allowance horses are a dime a dozen, but the first-class stakes horse is a precious commodity. At the same time, the stakes horse is usually the most combustible. A favorite saying among thoroughbred trainers is that they "never had a good horse who was a sound horse." As trainer Gary Jones observed, "The common horse will quit as soon as he feels the slightest pain. The good horse has the heart and the will to ignore the pain. He'll continue to put stress on his body, really lay it down, and that's when a horse gets hurt. The good ones don't know when to quit."

Since the best horses are so fragile, it makes sense to maximize their fleeting careers on the racetrack. No one has ever done it better for a single season than Whiteley in 1979.

To win all that money with so few starters, Whiteley had to pit his horses against the best opposition in the richest races. He won major events in New York, California, and Florida. His barn included a champion, a classic winner, two top turf runners, and a bunch of well-bred maidens running over with potential. These were the big guns in the arsenal:

—Tiller, owned by William Haggin Perry, defeated what is considered the finest San Juan Capistrano Handicap field in the last 20 years. Tiller's victims that day included Exceller, defending champion and winner of the 1978 Jockey Club Gold Cup; Noble Dancer, the international star who had beaten Tiller in their previous encounter; and State Dinner, subsequent winner of the Metropolitan Mile and Suburban Handicap in New York.

—Instrument Landing, unlike Tiller, loathed California. When he returned to New York, however, he immediately displayed his gratitude by upsetting General Assembly and Screen King in the Wood Memorial, returning $17.20 in the bargain.

—Waya was the best turf mare in the country in 1978 and early 1979. After she successfully carried 131 pounds in the March 25 Santa

Barbara Handicap at Santa Anita, a wise guy on the racetrack staff put out an April Fool's release announcing her retirement because her next assignment would be equivalent to the weight of a wide-screen television. Whiteley got a good laugh, then changed gears. Waya could handle the dirt just fine, too, and showed it by winning New York's Top Flight Handicap in the spring and Beldame Stakes in the fall. She was voted champion of all older mares.

—French Colonial picked up the slack during the summer when Tiller went lame in New York. His victories included the Knickerbocker Handicap. Not to be outdone, French Colonial's little sister Clef d'Argent won the Test Stakes at Saratoga.

—The real scene-stealer was Coastal, whose crooked foot disguised a tremendous staying power and competitive zeal. In any other year, Coastal would have been a champion, but he came along as a contemporary of Spectacular Bid and at the end of the Affirmed Era. Coastal won the Belmont Stakes to end the Triple Crown dreams of Spectacular Bid, and later in the year Coastal gave Affirmed a scare in the Woodward Stakes. Then, in October, Coastal helped make the Jockey Club Gold Cup "The Race of the Year" by finishing a close third to Affirmed and Spectacular Bid. With six wins in nine starts, Coastal's 1979 earnings represented 27 percent of the Whiteley total.

Ron and John

As with jockeys, every horseplayer has a favorite trainer. Ron McAnally would seem to be a natural for the kind of top 10 trainer group examined earlier in this chapter. Yet his numbers, even though statistically brilliant, are not what they seem.

McAnally is doomed to everlasting association with the Grand Old Man of Racing, John Henry. (Let's face it, that's not a bad way to spend eternity.)

But professional horsemen are rankled by the suggestion that they owe all of their fame and fortune to one horse. They resist becoming defined as limited, opportunistic, flashes in the pan. They prefer posterity to think of them first, and their horses later.

McAnally has become comfortable with his place in racing history as the man behind John Henry. A little digging will also show that other McAnally horses through the years performed well with regularity. He trained a horse with the heart of a pea, Super Moment, to win more than a million dollars. He tamed the brilliantly fast Pay Tribute, a high-strung basket case, long enough to win a Hollywood Gold Cup. In 1975 his horses won the Del Mar Debutante and Del Mar Handicap on the same weekend. John Henry was no accident.

McAnally fans may be wondering why he was not included in the select group of trainers examined earlier in this chapter. After all, McAnally ranked among the top 10 money-winners from 1980 through 1984 when his stable averaged $3,073,962 in purses. He never won the national title, but he was fourth, second, fifth, seventh, and third during those years.

The massive contribution by John Henry to the McAnally numbers throws everything out of sync. John Henry won $5,645,437 while trained by McAnally, a figure that represented 30.3 percent of the entire stable output for the years 1979–1984. Without John Henry, McAnally would have made the top 10 only twice, with the average Stable earnings falling below $2,000,000. In 1984 the disparity was especially dramatic. John Henry's earnings of $2,336,650 were 54 percent of the McAnally stable's total.

There are historical precedents for such an imbalance. In 1979 Spectacular Bid accounted for 49 percent of the $2,261,364 earned by the Buddy Delp stable. In 1967, Damascus was a one-man band for Frank Whiteley, winning 85 percent of the stable's $960,630 in prize money. Ross Fenstermaker started 177 horses in 1985 but Precisionist, racing only nine times, brought home 62% of the stable's $1,759,925 total. The epitome of the "lightning in a bottle" school of training also came in 1985 when Cam Gambolotti won $3,552,704 in seven starts with Spend a Buck and $151,176 in 107 starts by the rest of his horses. After Spend a Buck retired, Gambolatti disappeared.

Here's a look at the recent McAnally record, with John Henry's contributions isolated in a separate column:

Year	Stable Total	Ranking	John Henry Total—%
1979	$ 994,432	29th	$ 59,950—6.0%
1980	2,066,180	4th	650,600—31.4%
1981	3,767,092	2nd	1,359,850—36.1%
1982	2,788,897	5th	586,387—21.0%
1983	2,429,344	7th	652,100—26.8%
1984	4,314,968	4th	2,336,650—54.1%
1985	2,254,631	17th	————————

Note that, with the exception of 1984, John Henry's share of the stable total is far less than the examples of "one-horse" stables cited earlier, suggesting that other horses in the barn were carrying their weight. If historians choose to label McAnally a one-horse trainer, however, the facts will tend to back them up. So will peer and public perception. When McAnally edged Charlie Whittingham in balloting for the 1981 Eclipse Award among trainers, Whittingham moaned, "He did it all with just one horse! I had a whole stable full!"

McAnally must be judged, however, by a different set of rules. Michelangelo may have spent four years painting the ceiling of the Sistine Chapel, but when he was through he had given the world the ceiling of the Sistine Chapel. McAnally poured 25 years of experience into the training of John Henry, and the horse responded by becoming the greatest, most popular money-making machine in the history of the sport. For five years (actually seven, counting John Henry's attempted comebacks), McAnally sculpted a career unequaled in geographic variety, duration, and drama. Would John Henry have accomplished as much in other hands? Impossible to answer. But there is evidence showing that it was McAnally who found the key to John Henry's best performances.

John Henry was trained by five different men during his racing days. Each time he was turned over to a more successful horseman in a more advanced setting he ran better. But he saved his quantum leap for McAnally. All other variables—weather, age, surface—mean nothing alongside the unshakable impression that John Henry was always a great horse waiting to be treated like one.

The following table illustrates John Henry's progression from mediocrity to greatness as he moved from stable to stable:

Trainer	Starts	Wins	Earnings
Phil Marino	16	3	$ 50,353
Hal Snowden	1	0	425
Robert Donato	13	6	118,921
V. J. Nickerson	15	6	782,811
Ron McAnally	38	24	5,645,437
Totals	83	39	6,597,947

The first phase of his career was spent in Louisiana, where the racing (except on the very best days at Louisiana Downs and the Fair Grounds) lags behind the major leagues when it comes to feed, water, surface maintenance, and, most importantly, purses. John Henry ran

16 times under such conditions, winning only three races and less than $60,000.

Midway through 1978 John Henry became a New York horse with trainer Bobby Donato, who had never been near a national top 10. But give Donato credit for introducing John Henry to better living conditions and, more importantly, to turf racing. The horse loved both ideas. John Henry won 6 of 13 races for Donato, including two stakes, and tripled his previous earnings.

Victor "Lefty" Nickerson, a successful New Yorker whose dry, buttoned-down humor belies a passionate dedication to the game, took over in 1979. Nickerson immediately recognized John Henry's potential. He upped the ante, tossing John Henry in against some very tough competition. John Henry responded to the challenge by finishing second in the prestigious Sword Dancer Handicap at Belmont Park and winning two tough allowance races later in the season. Among those he beat were Waya, champion mare that year, and Told, a world-record setter on grass.

Nickerson gets all the credit for bringing McAnally into the picture. They were old friends back in Kentucky, and they had shared clients and referrals in the past. When Nickerson told owner Sam Rubin to send John Henry to McAnally in California, he immediately became horse racing's "Man Who Threw Away Millions."

During 1980, John Henry bounced back and forth between the coasts. In five races for Nickerson he won one, finished second three times, and was third once. In nine races for McAnally, John Henry won eight and was second in the other one. Rubin got the message.

John Henry spent the rest of his career based in California with McAnally. He became Horse of the Year in 1981 and 1984. His globetrotting took him from L.A. to New York to Chicago to San Francisco to Japan. From 1981 through 1984 John Henry started 30 times and won 18 races (15 of them rated Grade I). It was rumored that McAnally continued to share his percentage of John Henry's winnings (eventually more than $500,000) with Nickerson, who had nothing to do with the horse after the fall of 1980. McAnally would smile whenever he heard the story and say, "Everything I have and my family has today is because of John Henry. I got John Henry because of Lefty. Let's just say I've never forgotten that."

Conclusion

During the summer of my thirteenth year a horse by the name of Faye's Grandson was running at Del Mar. Neither Faye (my grandmother) nor her grandson (me) jumped at the obvious hunch bet. We were too smart, too sophisticated. Of course, the horse won, and won at a big price.

Ever since that day I have felt like a marked man. Horse racing put its hook in me, making me wiggle and squirm at the thought of its maddening inconsistencies. Writing this book has given me a way to quiet my sneaky demons—and put a coat of rationality on an otherwise irrational sport. In a world where a Faye's Grandson can happen, anything can happen. Once I accepted that, the rest came easily.

The 1986 racing season unfolded around me as I wrote. In many ways it proved to be a relatively unsurprising extension of the season (1985) I was studying. Lady's Secret, Snow Chief, Precisionist, Chris McCarron, William Mott and several others continued their high level of achievement without taking a breath between calendars. And there were many surprises—pleasant and otherwise—that serve as more recent examples of some of the phenomena analyzed in this book.

Among them were:

• The campaign of Capote, champion 2-year-old colt of 1986. It was a masterpiece of timing. Capote won only two stakes races, the fewest of any young champion since his sire, Seattle Slew, took the same title in 1976. But his first stakes victory was against New York star Gulch in an East-West showdown in the Norfolk Stakes, and his second was the Breeders' Cup Juvenile—where he beat the rest of the best of his division. That was all it took.

• Tiffany Lass, who won her title as best 3-year-old filly by going unbeaten in Louisiana, Arkansas, and Kentucky. That, plus a quarter, is usually enough to get you a phone call. But this time proved the exception. The field that Tiffany Lass beat in the Kentucky Oaks turned out to be the best assembled by the division all year long. Tiffany Lass proved that her perfect record against lesser lights was simply a preview of greatness.

• Pat Day. He won the most races of any jockey in North America for the fourth time in the last five years, once again mopping up on soft competition in the Midwest. He also won the coveted Eclipse Award over such New York and California standouts as Jose Santos, Gary Stevens, and Chris McCarron. Day's supporters pointed proudly to his 11 victories in Grade I stakes as positive proof that he excels at the highest levels. Only McCarron won as many. What they failed to mention, however, is that six of Day's 11 wins came aboard Lady's Secret, a push-button dynamo who needed little more than steering. McCarron's 11 Grade I wins came aboard 10 different horses.

• And 1986 gave us another muddled sprint division. Once again, the championship went to the winner of the Breeders' Cup Sprint . . . by default. Without a doubt, the victorious Smile was at his very best on Breeders' Cup day. But he had already been proven an inferior sprinter to a horse named Phone Trick. And Phone Trick's only loss came at the hands of the volatile Groovy. However, Groovy was beaten badly as the favorite in the Breeders' Cup Sprint, while Phone Trick missed the race because of an injury. Smile had the last, and loudest, word.

Horse racing is like any other complex subject: the more you know, the less you know. Breeders' Cup day in 1986 resulted in the greatest attack on sanity in the recent history of the sport. Five of the greatest stars of the era were *losers* on the same day at the same track. Precisionist, winner of more than $3,000,000—loser. Turkoman, the big colt with the freight train finish—loser. Sonic Lady, the English filly compared to the greats of the past—loser. Estrapade, a champion mare—loser. And Dancing Brave, considered by Europeans to be nothing less than the second coming of Pegasus—loser. Only little Lady's Secret escaped the 1986 Breeders' Cup Day Massacre. For that reason alone she may have deserved her title as 1986 Horse of the Year.

Perhaps we have found the ultimate measure of ability in horse racing, the quality for which we should all be searching. The handicapper, the historian, and the hardcore racing fan can be momentarily distracted by flash and style. But when they put their money down on horse, jockey, or trainer, they prize one creature over all the rest. They prize the survivor.

Good luck.

Index

About the Author

Jay Hovdey blames his grandmother, Faye Erickson, for his lifelong addiction to fast horses. His professors at Arizona State University probably thought they were training a fresh-faced cub reporter. After three years in the publicity departments of Del Mar, Hollywood Park, and Santa Anita, he went to work for the Los Angeles edition of the *Daily Racing Form* and became assistant to the editor.

Since 1975 he has written for a variety of thoroughbred racing trade journals, and in 1982 he won an Eclipse award for his story about the champion filly Landaluce, which appeared in *The Horseman's Journal*.

His work has also appeared in *The New York Times, The Los Angeles Times, The Baltimore Sun, The Houston Post, The Fort Worth Star-Telegram, The Thoroughbred Record, The Thoroughbred of California, Spur Magazine, Gaming & Wagering Business, Blood-Horse of New Zealand, The European Racehorse*, and *Pacemaker International*, England's leading thoroughbred magazine.

In 1984 he hung out his shingle as a free-lance writer and racing consultant. His clients have included Breeder's Cup, Ltd. and the Oak Tree Racing Association. He recently began managing the California campaign of an English racehorse.

His wife, Suzanne, is an executive with American Medical International, and his son, Eddie, is a natural in the saddle.

Printed in the United States
by Baker & Taylor Publisher Services